MALTA & GOZO
GUIDE 2025

Uncovering Hidden Gems

David S. Harden

Copyright © 2025.

All rights reserved. No part of this publication may be reproduced, distributed, or transmitted in any form or by any means, including photocopying, recording, or other electronic or mechanical methods, without the prior written permission of the publisher, except in the case of brief quotations embodied in critical reviews and certain other noncommercial uses permitted by copyright law

Table of contents

Introduction to Malta and Gozo
    Geography and Climate
    A Brief History
    Cultural Traditions and Customs
    Language Basics for Travelers
    Essential Travel Information
Key Cities and Towns
    Malta
        Valletta
        St. Julian's
        Mdina
        Rabat
        Marsaxlokk
        Mellieha
        Qormi
        Birkirkara
        Birgu
        Senglea
        Cospicua
    Gozo
        Victoria
        Xlendi
        Marsalforn
Historical & Cultural Gems

- Ancient Temples and Sites
- UNESCO World Heritage Sites
- Fortresses and Citadels
- Museums and Art Galleries
- Festivals and Local Events

Outdoor Adventures
- National Parks and Reserves
- Hiking and Walking Trails
- Water Sports and Beach Activities
- Diving and Snorkeling Spots
- Wildlife and Nature Tours

Maltese Cuisine
- Must-Try Dishes and Desserts
- Wine Regions and Local Breweries
- Farmers' Markets and Food Tours
- Cooking Classes and Workshops
- Dining Etiquette Tips

Transportation & Stays
- Ferries and Inter-Island Travel
- Public Transport: Buses and Taxis
- Car Rentals and Road Trips
- Accommodation Options
- Unique Lodging Experiences

Travel Tips & Safety
- Best Seasons to Visit

- Budgeting and Saving Money
- Health and Safety Advice
- Cultural Do's and Don'ts

Shopping & Souvenirs
- Traditional Crafts and Lacework
- Best Markets and Shopping Streets
- Local Delicacies to Bring Home
- Antique and Vintage Hunting
- Ethical Shopping Guide

Nightlife and Hidden Gems
- Popular Nightclubs and Bars
- Live Music and Entertainment
- Secluded Spots and Nature Trails
- Unique Local Experiences
- Quaint Villages and Walks

Trip Planning
- 7-Day Itinerary for First-Timers
- Family-Friendly Activities

Conclusion

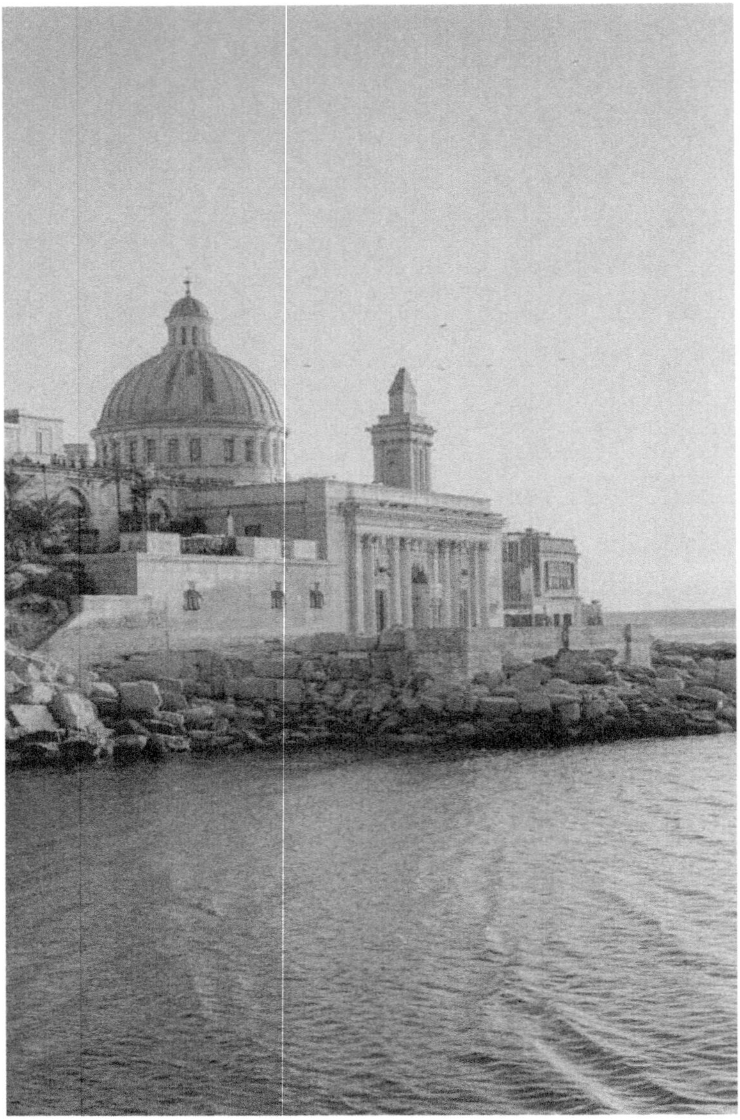

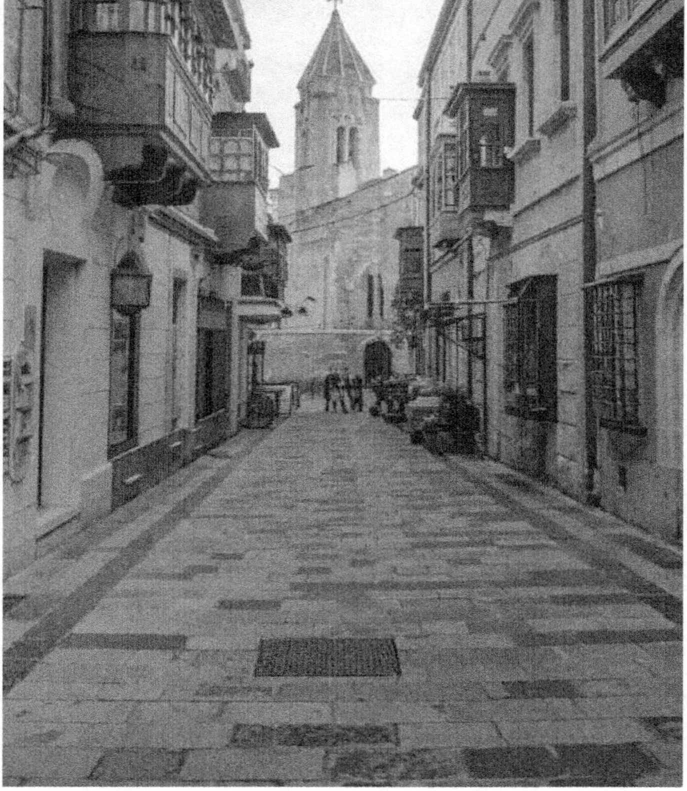

8

Introduction to Malta and Gozo

There are places you visit and forget, and then there are places that imprint themselves on your soul. Malta and Gozo belong to the latter. My journey to these Mediterranean islands wasn't just about sightseeing—it was an immersion into history, culture, and breathtaking landscapes that I will never forget.

The moment my plane landed at Malta International Airport, I knew I was in for something special. The warm Mediterranean air carried a hint of sea salt and history, whispering stories of ancient civilizations. I had read about Malta's past, but seeing it firsthand was something else entirely.

Valletta, the capital, was my first stop. Walking through the city felt like stepping into a living museum. Every street was lined with honey-colored limestone buildings, adorned with colorful wooden balconies. I explored St. John's Co-Cathedral, where the opulent Baroque interiors left me speechless. The marble floor, covered with intricate tombstones of the Knights of St. John, felt like a tribute to centuries of valor and sacrifice.

Later, I wandered down to the Grand Harbour. Watching the sun set behind the fortified walls, painting the sky in shades of orange and pink, was magical. A traditional Maltese pastizzi (flaky pastry filled with ricotta) in hand, I took in the view, wondering how many sailors and traders had gazed upon the same waters throughout history.

The next day, I visited Mdina, Malta's ancient capital. Known as the "Silent City," its narrow alleys and medieval architecture transported me back in time. The quiet streets, occasionally interrupted by the clip-clop of horse-drawn carriages, made me feel as if I were in a fairytale.

I stopped at Fontanella Tea Garden, famous for its panoramic views and delectable cakes. Sipping on a Maltese coffee while overlooking the vast countryside, I reflected on how well Malta preserves its past while embracing modernity.

After two days of exploring Malta, I took the ferry to Gozo. The short ride across the Mediterranean was refreshing, with seagulls soaring above and the clear blue waters shimmering under the sun.

Gozo felt different—quieter, greener, and more rural. The pace was slower, and the people seemed even more laid-back. I rented a bike and cycled through rolling hills, past rustic farmhouses, and picturesque villages.

One of my most memorable stops was the Ġgantija Temples, a UNESCO World Heritage Site older than the Pyramids of Egypt. As I stood before these massive stone structures, built by unknown hands over 5,500 years ago, I marveled at the ingenuity of our ancestors.

No trip to Gozo would be complete without visiting Dwejra. Although the famous Azure Window had collapsed, the area's natural beauty remained breathtaking. I took a boat tour through the Blue Hole and into sea caves, where the water was an unbelievable shade of blue.

As I snorkeled in the crystal-clear waters, I felt an overwhelming sense of connection to nature. Schools of fish darted past me, and the underwater rock formations created an almost surreal world beneath the waves.

Food in Malta and Gozo was an adventure of its own. Every meal was a delight, from fresh seafood in Marsaxlokk to rabbit stew (fenek), a traditional Maltese delicacy. I learned that Maltese cuisine is a reflection of the island's history—Arab, Italian, British, and French influences blended into unique flavors.

On my last evening, I dined at a local family-run restaurant in Gozo. The owner, an elderly Gozitan man, shared stories of his youth and how the island had changed over the decades. As I savored my plate of lampuki (dolphinfish) with sun-dried tomatoes and capers, I realized that travel isn't just about places—it's about people and their stories.

As I took the ferry back to Malta for my flight home, I looked at the islands one last time, knowing I'd return someday. Malta and Gozo had given me more than just beautiful sights—they had offered me a lesson in history, resilience, and the art of enjoying life at a slower pace.

Traveling here wasn't just a vacation; it was an experience that stayed with me long after I left. Whether it was exploring ancient ruins, swimming in turquoise waters, or sharing a meal with locals, every moment had been a memory in the making.

And that, I realized, is the beauty of Malta and Gozo. They don't just welcome visitors; they embrace them, whispering tales of the past while inviting them to create their own.

Geography and Climate

Malta is an archipelago in the central Mediterranean, about 93 km south of Sicily and 290 km north of Libya. It consists of three main islands: Malta, Gozo, and Comino. Malta is the largest and most developed, home to the capital, Valletta, and most of the population. Gozo is more rural, with terraced fields, traditional villages, and limestone cliffs. Comino, the smallest, is largely uninhabited but famous for the Blue Lagoon. The islands have a limestone terrain, rocky coastlines, and a few small sandy beaches. There are no mountains or rivers, though valleys and ridges shape the landscape. The highest point in Malta is Ta' Dmejrek at 253 meters.

Malta and Gozo have a Mediterranean climate, with hot, dry summers and mild, wet winters. Summers, from June to September, bring temperatures between 30–35°C, with high humidity and occasional heatwaves. Autumn, from October to November, is warm with increasing rainfall and occasional storms. Winters, from December to February, are mild but wet, with temperatures ranging from 10–18°C. Strong winds, particularly the gregale from the northeast, can bring rough seas. Spring, from March to May, is pleasant, with highs between 17–25°C and low rainfall.

Rainfall is concentrated between October and March, averaging 500–600 mm per year, while summers are mostly dry. The islands are often windy, affected by the hot, dusty sirocco from North Africa and the cooler mistral from the northwest. The surrounding Mediterranean waters remain warm for most of the year, with sea temperatures ranging from 24–27°C in summer and 15–17°C in winter, making Malta and Gozo popular for swimming, diving, and water sports.

A Brief History

Malta and Gozo sit right in the middle of the Mediterranean, a small but strategically significant cluster of islands about 93 kilometers south of Sicily and 290 kilometers north of Libya. Malta, the largest and busiest of the three main islands, is where most of the action happens. It's home to Valletta, the historic capital, and a coastline that swings between dramatic cliffs, rocky inlets, and a handful of sandy beaches. Gozo, its smaller, quieter neighbor, moves at a different pace. Life there is more rural, with rolling terraced fields, traditional stone farmhouses, and sleepy villages where time seems to stretch a little longer. Then there's Comino, a tiny, mostly uninhabited island wedged between the two. Its main claim to fame is the Blue Lagoon, a sheltered stretch of neon-blue water that draws tourists by the boatload in summer. Beyond that, it's just a handful of walking trails, a single hotel, and a lot of rugged limestone landscape.

The geography of the islands is shaped almost entirely by limestone, which dictates not just the terrain but also the way the towns look. The honey-colored stone used to build Valletta, Mdina, and the smaller villages comes straight from the land itself. There are no mountains, no rivers, and very little forest—just rolling hills, rocky outcrops, and a network of valleys that carve through the landscape. The highest point, Ta' Dmejrek, barely scrapes 253 meters, so you won't find any dramatic peaks here. What you do get are sweeping coastal views, sheer cliffs that plunge straight into the sea, and a series of small, sheltered bays where the water is calm and impossibly clear.

The climate is classic Mediterranean—long, hot summers and short, mild winters. Between June and September, temperatures often climb above 30°C, with July and August being the hottest months. Humidity can make it feel even warmer, especially in the built-up areas where the limestone buildings absorb the heat. Rain is almost non-existent in summer, but by late autumn, things start to shift. October and November bring more unsettled weather, with short but heavy bursts of rain and the occasional thunderstorm. Winter, which runs from December to February, is mild by European standards, with temperatures ranging between 10–18°C. Snow is unheard of, but strong winds, especially the gregale—a powerful northeasterly that whips through the islands a few times each winter—can make it feel colder than it is.

Spring, from March to May, is one of the best times to be here. The temperatures hover in the comfortable range of 17–25°C, and the landscape, which turns dry and dusty in summer, is at its greenest. The wildflowers bloom, the countryside is dotted with patches of bright yellow mustard plants, and the air is crisp but warm. It's also when the sea starts to warm up again after the winter months, hitting around 17°C in April before climbing steadily through summer. By July and August, the water reaches a balmy 27°C, making it perfect for swimming, snorkeling, and diving. Even in the cooler months, the sea rarely drops below 15°C, which means you can swim year-round if you don't mind a bit of a chill.

The winds are another defining feature of Malta's climate. The islands sit right in the path of several strong Mediterranean winds, each bringing its own distinct weather. The sirocco, a hot, dry wind from North Africa, sometimes rolls in carrying Saharan dust, turning the sky a hazy orange and coating everything in a fine layer of sand. On the other hand, the mistral, which sweeps down from the northwest, is a cooling wind that clears the air and brings crisp, bright days. The maestrale, another northwesterly wind, often brings rough seas, making it a challenge for fishermen and sailors.

Malta's history runs as deep as its limestone quarries. The islands have been inhabited for more than 7,000 years, and some of the world's oldest freestanding structures can be found here. The megalithic temples at Ħaġar Qim, Mnajdra, and Ġgantija in Gozo predate both the Egyptian pyramids and Stonehenge, built by a civilization that left behind elaborate carvings and a complex religious structure but no written records. Later came the Phoenicians, the seafaring traders who gave the islands their first taste of international commerce. The Romans followed, and after them, the Arabs, whose influence is still felt in the Maltese language—a unique blend of Arabic, Italian, and English.

The most famous rulers of Malta, though, were the Knights of St. John. Granted the islands in 1530, they transformed Malta into a heavily fortified stronghold, building Valletta from scratch after the Great Siege of 1565. Their legacy is visible everywhere—in the grand palaces, the imposing bastions, and the intricate churches that fill the islands. The British took over in the early 19th century, and Malta remained a key naval base for over 150 years. It played a crucial role in World War

II, withstanding relentless bombing during the Siege of Malta, before finally gaining independence in 1964.

Cultural Traditions and Customs

Malta and Gozo have a cultural identity shaped by centuries of foreign rule, religious devotion, and a strong sense of community. Despite their small size, these islands have a rich blend of European, Middle Eastern, and Mediterranean influences, creating a culture that is both unique and deeply rooted in tradition.

Religion plays a central role in everyday life, and Catholicism is more than just a faith here—it's a way of life. Every town and village has its own parish church, often grander than you'd expect for the size of the community. The church dominates the skyline, and its bells mark the rhythm of the day. Many Maltese people attend Mass regularly, and religious holidays are taken seriously. Easter and Christmas are particularly important, with elaborate processions, reenactments, and late-night church services. During Easter, towns hold **sette giorni**—seven days of religious events leading up to Good Friday. Statues of Christ and the Virgin Mary are carried through the streets, often by men walking barefoot in an act of devotion.

But if you really want to see Malta's religious fervor in full swing, visit during **village festas**. These local feasts, dedicated to a town's patron saint, are among the liveliest and most colorful events in the Maltese calendar. Every village has its own festa, usually held between May and September. Streets are decorated with banners and lights, marching bands fill the air with music, and the church at the center of town becomes the focal point of days-long celebrations. The highlight is always the fireworks—Maltese pyrotechnics are among the best in the world, and many villages compete to put on the most spectacular show. Alongside the religious ceremonies, festas are also about food, drink, and socializing. Street vendors sell **pastizzi** (flaky pastries stuffed with ricotta or mushy peas), nougat, and grilled meats, while locals gather outside bars and restaurants, sipping on local beer or a shot of **Bajtra**, a sweet prickly pear liqueur.

Beyond religious events, family and community are at the heart of Maltese society. The islands are small, and people tend to know their neighbors well. Extended families remain close, and Sunday lunches are almost sacred—multi-generational gatherings where tables overflow with homemade dishes like **rabbit stew (fenkata)**, **kapunata** (Maltese ratatouille), and **bragioli** (beef rolls stuffed with bacon and herbs). Hospitality is deeply ingrained in Maltese culture, and if you're invited into a local home, you'll be encouraged to eat more than you can handle. Saying no isn't really an option.

Gozo, while sharing many of the same traditions as Malta, has always had a slightly more rural and traditional character. The island has a strong agricultural background, and its customs are deeply tied to the land. One of the oldest traditions still alive in Gozo is **l-għana**, a form of Maltese folk singing. This isn't just music—it's a form of improvised poetry, where two singers engage in a playful battle of words, often weaving social commentary and humor into their verses. This tradition, once common across Malta, has survived most strongly in Gozo's small villages.

Another deeply rooted tradition across both islands is **carnival**, which dates back centuries and is celebrated with enthusiasm in February. Valletta hosts the biggest and most organized event, featuring extravagant floats, costumes, and street parties. But for something wilder and more bizarre, head to **Nadur in Gozo**, where carnival takes on a darker, more satirical tone. Locals dress in eerie, grotesque costumes, mocking politicians and society in a way that feels more like a masked rebellion than a festival.

Superstition also plays a role in Maltese culture. Despite being a deeply religious nation, many Maltese still hold onto old beliefs passed down through generations. It's not uncommon for people to hang a small horn-shaped charm called a **għajn**, meant to ward off the evil eye, especially in newborn babies' cribs. Some fishermen still paint the traditional **Luzzu boats** with a pair of eyes on the bow, an ancient Phoenician tradition believed to protect them from harm at sea.

Traditional crafts are still valued, though modern life has made them less common. Gozo is known for its **lace-making**, a delicate and intricate skill that has been passed down for generations. Older women can sometimes still be seen sitting outside their doorsteps, meticulously weaving lace with bobbins and pins. Another craft unique to Malta is **filigree jewelry**, made from delicate strands of silver or gold twisted into intricate patterns, often depicting religious symbols or Maltese crosses.

One of the most enduring elements of Maltese culture is its language. **Maltese** is the only Semitic language written in Latin script, a fusion of Arabic, Italian, and a sprinkling of English. It's a linguistic reflection of Malta's history, shaped by centuries of trade, conquest, and migration. While English is widely spoken—Malta was a British colony until 1964—Maltese remains the language of everyday life, spoken in homes, markets, and village squares.

Despite modernization, Malta and Gozo have managed to hold onto their traditions in a way that few places do. The festas, the Sunday lunches, the folk music, and even the old superstitions continue to thrive, not as relics of the past but as a living part of everyday life. This is a place where history isn't just found in museums—it's woven into the fabric of the islands, in the rhythms of daily life, and in the way people gather, celebrate, and tell their stories.

Language Basics for Travelers

Maltese is the national language of Malta, and it stands out as the only Semitic language written in the Latin alphabet. While its base comes from Arabic, centuries of influence from Italian, Sicilian, and English have shaped it into something distinct. English is also an official language and widely spoken, particularly in tourist areas, but making an effort to use a few Maltese words can go a long way in connecting with locals. They appreciate it when visitors show an interest in their language, even if it's just a simple greeting or thank you.

A casual way to say hello in Maltese is "Bongu," though many people also use "Ciao" or simply "Hello." For something more traditional, "Merħba" means welcome. Politeness is valued in Malta, so "Grazzi" is the go-to word for thank you, and "Jekk jogħġbok" means please. If someone thanks you, replying with "M'hemmx problema" is a common way of saying no problem. When ordering something or making a request, "Nista'...?" means "Can I...?" so asking for a coffee would be "Nista' jkolli kafè?" If you need to answer a yes or no question, "Iva" means yes, and "Le" means no.

When meeting someone, "Kif int?" is the way to ask how they are. If addressing more than one person or being polite, "Kif intom?" is the correct form. The standard response is "Tajjeb, grazzi" for men and "Tajba, grazzi" for women, meaning "Good, thanks." Asking for someone's name is as simple as saying "X'jismek?" and to introduce yourself, you can say "Jien…" followed by your name.

Getting around in Malta is relatively easy, but knowing a few words can make things smoother. Asking for directions starts with "Fejn hu...?" meaning "Where is...?" so "Fejn hu l-ajruport?" would mean "Where is the airport?" If looking for the capital, you'd ask "Fejn hu l-belt Valletta?" Public transport is widely used, and if you need to know departure times, "X'ħin jitlaq it-trasport?" means "What time does the transport leave?" In a taxi, asking "Kemm se jiswa?" will get you the price.

Food is a big part of Maltese culture, and ordering in a restaurant or café is a great chance to try using the language. "Nixtieq..." means "I would like…," so if you want to order a drink, you'd say "Nixtieq xarba," or if you're looking for a classic Maltese snack, you could ask for "Nixtieq platt tal-pastizzi." In most tourist areas, English is widely used in restaurants, but locals always appreciate the effort when visitors try a bit of Maltese.

While Malta is a safe country, it's always good to know a few emergency phrases just in case. If you need immediate help, "Għinni!" means "Help me!" If calling the police, you'd say "Sejjaħ lill-pulizija!" and if a doctor is needed, "Għandi bżonn tabib" will get the point across. If something is urgent, saying "Huwa urġenti!" makes it clear that it's serious.

Maltese expressions can be fun to learn, and they add a bit of local color to conversations. One of the most commonly heard phrases is "Mela!" which doesn't have a direct translation but is often used like "of course" or "obviously." "Ejja ħa mmorru!" means "Come on, let's go!" and is something you might hear from an impatient bus driver or a friend trying to hurry you along. Because of the long-standing Italian influence, many Maltese people casually slip in Italian words. "Allura" is one of the most common—it means something like "so" or "well then." And while Maltese is the everyday language, English words have found their way into daily conversations, particularly among younger generations.

The language itself is a reflection of Malta's long and layered history. It started as a dialect of Arabic, shaped by North African traders and settlers, before absorbing Italian and Sicilian vocabulary through centuries of trade and cultural exchange. When the Knights of St. John arrived, they brought Latin and French influences, and British rule in the 19th and 20th centuries added English to the mix. Today, while many Maltese people are bilingual and use English for business and tourism, Maltese remains the language of daily life. Walking through a market or sitting in a village square, you'll hear a mix of Maltese and English, sometimes even within the same sentence.

Even though English is widely understood, knowing a few Maltese words can make a difference in how you experience the islands. Locals are used to tourists speaking English, but when someone makes the effort to say "Grazzi" or "Bongu," it's always met with appreciation.

Essential Travel Information

Malta and Gozo may be small, but there are a few things travelers should know to make their trip smoother. The islands are well-connected, easy to navigate, and packed with history, but understanding transportation, currency, safety, and a few local customs can go a long way in ensuring a hassle-free visit.

Malta International Airport (MLA) is the country's only airport, located in Luqa, about a 20-minute drive from Valletta. Most international flights arrive here, and from the airport, you can take taxis, rental cars, or buses to different parts of the island. There's no railway system, so buses are the main form of public transport. They're affordable, but they can be slow and crowded, especially in peak summer months. For those staying in Valletta, the ferry to Sliema or the Three Cities is a great alternative to buses. To reach Gozo, travelers need to take the Gozo Channel ferry from Ċirkewwa, which runs frequently throughout the day. There's also a fast ferry from Valletta to Gozo, cutting down travel time significantly.

The currency in Malta is the euro (€), and credit cards are widely accepted in hotels, restaurants, and larger shops. However, in smaller villages, at local markets, or on the Gozo ferry, it's good to have some cash on hand. ATMs are easy to find, especially in tourist areas. Tipping isn't compulsory, but in restaurants, rounding up the bill or leaving 5–10% is appreciated. In taxis, rounding up the fare is common, and for hotel staff or tour guides, a small tip is a nice gesture but not expected.

Malta is generally very safe, with a low crime rate and a strong police presence in tourist areas. Petty theft isn't common, but as in any destination, it's wise to be aware of your belongings, particularly in crowded areas like Valletta, Sliema, and popular beaches. Roads can be narrow and winding, and driving is on the left side, a remnant of British rule. Traffic can be heavy, especially in and around Valletta, so renting a car is only recommended for those comfortable with tight streets and aggressive local drivers. If you prefer not to drive, taxis and ride-hailing apps like Bolt are widely available.

Malta's healthcare system is reliable, with well-equipped hospitals and clinics. EU citizens can use their European Health Insurance Card (EHIC) for emergency treatment, while other visitors are advised to have travel insurance. Pharmacies are common and well-stocked, with many medications available over the counter that might require a prescription elsewhere. Tap water is technically safe to drink, but many locals and visitors prefer bottled water due to its taste.

The best time to visit Malta depends on what you're looking for. Summer, from June to September, is the hottest and busiest season, with temperatures often exceeding 30°C. This is peak time for beachgoers, festival lovers, and nightlife seekers. Spring (March to May) and autumn (October to November) offer warm weather without the summer crowds, making them ideal for sightseeing and outdoor activities. Winter is mild, with temperatures rarely dropping below 10°C, and while some tourist sites have shorter hours, it's a good time for those looking for a quieter experience.

Power outlets in Malta use the British-style three-pin plug (Type G), so travelers from mainland Europe or North America may need an adapter. Wi-Fi is widely available in hotels, cafés, and restaurants, and mobile data coverage is excellent across both Malta and Gozo. EU travelers can use their phones without roaming charges, but visitors from outside Europe should check with their provider before using data services.

Malta has a relaxed but respectful approach to dress and behavior. While beachwear is fine along the coast, covering up in churches and religious sites is expected. Maltese people are friendly and welcoming, but public displays of affection, particularly in rural areas, are more reserved compared to other European countries. The Maltese schedule runs a little later than some visitors might be used to—dinner typically starts around 8 pm, and nightlife picks up even later.

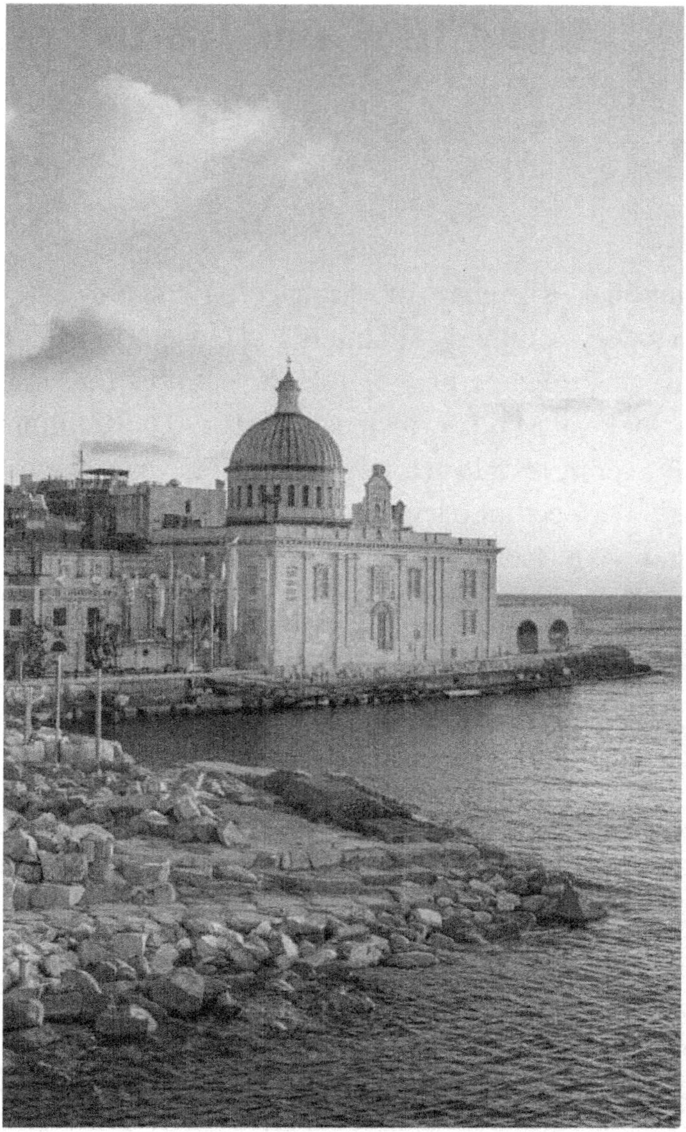

Key Cities and Towns

Malta

Valletta

The National Museum of Archaeology stands as one of Valletta's key cultural landmarks. Housed in the historic Auberge de Provence on Republic Street, this museum offers a close look at Malta's ancient heritage. The building itself, with its centuries-old stone walls, sets the stage for an impressive collection of prehistoric artifacts, pottery, and tools that chart the island's early human activity. Visitors are welcome from 9:00 AM until 5:00 PM, except on Tuesdays when the museum remains closed. The entry fee is around €10 for adults, with concessions available for students and seniors at roughly €6, while children under 12 enter free.

A short stroll from this treasure trove of antiquity brings you to MUZA, the National Museum of Fine Arts. This institution brings together classic works and modern pieces in a refreshing display of artistic evolution. The building, a blend of contemporary design and historic touches, sits within easy reach of the city center. MUZA opens its doors at 10:00 AM and closes at 6:00 PM, taking a day off on Mondays. Admission is priced at approximately €12 for adults, with reduced rates for seniors and students, making it a compelling stop for those who appreciate both tradition and innovation in art.

Not far away, the Palace Armoury within the Grand Master's Palace on Republic Street invites visitors to experience a slice of Malta's military past. Once the seat of the Knights of Malta, the palace now offers a display of historical weaponry and armor that tells stories of courage and conflict. The exhibits are arranged to give context to each artifact, drawing clear connections between the objects and the turbulent eras they represent. Open from 10:00 AM to 4:30 PM, the Palace Armoury charges an admission fee of around €8 for adults, with discounted rates available for younger visitors and students.

For those interested in the vibrant pulse of Valletta's contemporary art scene, Spazju Kreattiv is a must-visit venue. More than a gallery, this creative space serves as a community hub for local artists and performers. Located near Old Mint Street, Spazju Kreattiv hosts a rotating schedule of exhibitions, live performances, and workshops that capture the evolving spirit of the city. The center welcomes visitors from 10:00 AM until 7:00 PM daily, and most events here are free of charge. The relaxed atmosphere makes it a favorite among locals and tourists alike, offering an accessible glimpse into Malta's modern cultural expressions.

Another engaging venue is the City Gate Arts Centre, which curates an eclectic mix of installations, photography, and multimedia presentations. The centre reflects the diverse artistic voices of Malta, blending influences from the island's rich traditions with global contemporary trends. Its central location in Valletta makes it easy to incorporate a visit into a day of cultural exploration. The centre typically operates from 11:00 AM to 6:00 PM, and entry is free, inviting anyone with a curiosity for art to step in and enjoy the creative offerings.

These institutions not only preserve the heritage of Malta but also celebrate its ongoing cultural evolution. In Valletta, each museum and gallery tells a part of the city's story—from ancient civilizations and chivalric orders to modern creative movements. The relatively close proximity of these venues allows for a leisurely day of discovery, where the past and present mingle along cobbled streets and sunlit courtyards.

As you wander through Valletta, the atmosphere is both reflective and invigorating. One moment you're absorbing the quiet reverence of ancient relics, and the next you're drawn into lively discussions at a contemporary gallery. The blend of historical depth and creative innovation is a reminder that

Valletta's culture is as dynamic as it is storied. Every exhibit, every carefully preserved artifact, and every modern installation contributes to a broader narrative that is uniquely Maltese.

Practical details are designed with the visitor in mind. Museums like the National Museum of Archaeology and the Palace Armoury offer clear schedules and affordable entry fees, ensuring that you can plan your day without any hassle. Meanwhile, contemporary spaces such as MUZA and Spazju Kreattiv often host temporary exhibitions or events, so it's worth checking their websites or local listings for any special programs during your visit.

Walking between these sites is part of the experience. Valletta's compact size and pedestrian-friendly streets mean that you can enjoy the journey as much as the destinations themselves. Each step along the way is accompanied by the sounds of daily life in a city that has long been a crossroads of culture and history.

Sliema
Fort Tigné stands as one of Sliema's intriguing cultural spots. Perched at Tigné Point along the waterfront, this historic fort has transformed from a military installation into a venue that

occasionally hosts exhibitions focused on local history and art. The sturdy stone walls and open courtyards speak of Malta's layered past, and its coastal setting means you can enjoy panoramic sea views while exploring its small displays. Typically, the fort welcomes visitors on weekends from 10:00 AM to 4:00 PM, and entry is free, though special events may call for a modest fee. Its location makes it an easy stop during a leisurely walk along the promenade.

Over on Tower Road, the Sliema Cultural Centre provides a warm setting for art and community. Housed in a renovated building that still hints at its original character, the centre hosts rotating exhibitions that cover everything from local photography to modern painting and sculpture. Visitors can drop in between 10:00 AM and 6:00 PM from Monday through Saturday, with a slightly later opening at 11:00 AM on Sundays. The space is free to enter, though occasional workshops or themed events might ask for a small contribution of around €5 to €10. The centre's inviting atmosphere makes it a popular gathering spot for both locals and visitors keen on experiencing the pulse of Maltese creativity.

Not far from the bustle of the main streets, Bayview Art Gallery offers a quiet retreat along Balluta Bay. With its large windows framing views of the Mediterranean, the gallery creates a relaxed environment for enjoying a curated selection of contemporary art. The exhibitions here change regularly, featuring a mix of established and emerging local talent. Open daily from 11:00 AM to 7:00 PM, Bayview Art Gallery welcomes art lovers with free entry, making it an accessible highlight during an afternoon stroll along Sliema's scenic waterfront.

Adding another layer to the local art scene, Urban Canvas Gallery occupies a renovated space on 32 St. Julian's Road. This venue showcases more experimental works that push the boundaries of conventional art, from urban photography to avant-garde installations. The raw, industrial feel of the space contrasts with the refined pieces on display, sparking conversations about the evolving nature of art on the island. Urban Canvas Gallery typically opens its doors at 10:00 AM and stays open until 7:00 PM, with no admission fee, allowing visitors to wander freely through its thought-provoking exhibitions.

St. Julian's

In St. Julian's, the Malta Aviation Museum offers a fascinating journey through the skies of the island's history. Located just a short distance from the vibrant nightlife of Paceville, this museum provides a unique look at Malta's role in aviation from World War II to the modern era. The collection includes a range of aircraft, from military planes to civilian models, all meticulously preserved. The museum opens daily from 10:00 AM to 4:00 PM, with a modest entrance fee of €10 for adults, and €5 for children and students. It's an ideal spot for anyone interested in the technical side of history, and its quiet location allows for a relaxed, immersive experience.

The National Museum of Fine Arts, not far from the bustling bay area, showcases an impressive collection of Maltese and international artwork. This gallery, which combines the works of renowned painters and local artists, is housed in a 19th-century building that adds a sense of grandeur to the exhibits. Open from 10:00 AM to 6:00 PM, the museum charges an entry fee of €7 for adults, with discounts available for seniors and students. It's a must-visit for art enthusiasts keen on discovering the artistic heart of Malta while enjoying the elegant surroundings of this charming space.

For something a little more contemporary, the St. Julian's Art Gallery, situated in the heart of the town, presents a dynamic collection of modern works by local artists. The gallery often features new exhibitions that reflect the evolving art scene in Malta, ranging from abstract pieces to thought-provoking installations. Open daily from 10:30 AM to 7:00 PM, with free entry, it's a great place to explore the fresh ideas coming out of the local creative community. It's an accessible spot for those looking to experience the cutting edge of Maltese art without the formality of larger institutions.

Tucked away in a quieter corner of St. Julian's, the Art of Living Gallery combines art with lifestyle, offering a curated collection of art pieces that explore the intersections of culture, design, and everyday life. This intimate space hosts a variety of exhibitions, focusing on both traditional and contemporary Maltese art. Open from 11:00 AM to 6:00 PM, the gallery provides a welcoming atmosphere where visitors can explore art while enjoying the relaxing vibe of the neighborhood. Entrance is free, and the gallery often organizes small events and workshops, making it a great place to engage directly with the local art scene.

Mdina

The Mdina Dungeons, located within the ancient city's stone walls, offers a gripping walk through the darker side of Malta's history. Set on Villegaignon Street, the museum is housed in a former prison and takes visitors on a journey through the island's medieval past, with life-like displays and eerie exhibits that highlight Malta's history of crime, punishment, and intrigue. It's a fascinating way to explore the island's tumultuous history, providing a stark contrast to the calm, quiet streets of Mdina. The museum is open daily from 9:30 AM to 5:30 PM, with an entry fee of €8 for adults and €5 for children. It's a perfect stop for those looking for a touch of history with a bit of a thrill.

The Palazzo Falson Historic House Museum, on the other hand, offers a refined look at Malta's noble past. Situated on Villegaignon Street, this museum resides in a 16th-century palazzo and displays the lavish lifestyle of the island's aristocracy. The museum's collection is diverse, showcasing everything from period furniture and antique clocks to fine art and rare manuscripts. A visit here is like stepping back in time, allowing you to explore the life of the noble Falson family. It's open Tuesday to Saturday from 10:00 AM to 4:30 PM, with a modest fee of €10 for adults and €5 for students and seniors. This museum is a must-see for those interested in Maltese aristocratic history and antique collections.

For art lovers, the Mdina Glass studio offers a more hands-on experience. A short walk from the city's central square, the glass factory and gallery showcase the delicate craftsmanship of Malta's famed glassmakers. The glass pieces displayed are vibrant and diverse, with intricate designs that represent both traditional and contemporary art forms. Visitors can watch artisans at work and learn about the centuries-old techniques used to create these stunning works. Mdina Glass is open daily from 9:30 AM to 5:30 PM, and while entry is free, purchasing a piece of the beautifully crafted glassware is a popular souvenir option. It's a wonderful way to take a piece of Mdina's artistic heritage home with you.

If you're looking to dive into Malta's archaeological past, the National Museum of Natural History is an excellent choice. Located in the heart of Mdina at the historic Villegaignon Palace, this museum offers exhibits on both Malta's natural world and its prehistoric origins. From fossils and geological specimens to an exploration of the island's unique wildlife, the museum gives a comprehensive view of the forces that shaped Malta. It's open from 9:00 AM to 5:00 PM daily, with an entry fee of €5 for adults and €3 for children. The museum's location within Mdina's medieval walls adds to the sense of stepping back in time, as it's housed in a building that itself holds centuries of history.

In Mdina, the museums and galleries present a diverse range of experiences, from the darker corners of history at the Mdina Dungeons to the opulent world of the Palazzo Falson. The town's well-preserved buildings and narrow streets offer the perfect setting for immersing yourself in the island's rich cultural heritage.

Rabat

The Wignacourt Museum, located in the heart of Rabat, is a must-see for anyone interested in the rich historical tapestry of Malta. Situated at 137 St. Paul Street, this museum is housed in the former residence of the Wignacourt Knights and offers a fascinating mix of religious and historical artifacts. The collection spans centuries, with displays ranging from sculptures, paintings, and antiques to a series of captivating archaeological finds that reveal Malta's ancient past. The museum also includes a charming garden and a selection of medieval relics. It's open Monday through Saturday from 9:30 AM to 5:00 PM, with an entry fee of €5 for adults and €3 for children. A visit here provides a unique opportunity to experience the intersection of Malta's religious and cultural history in a beautifully preserved setting.

Just a short walk away, the Domus Romana offers a striking glimpse into Malta's Roman past. Located on the main street in Rabat, this site was once a wealthy Roman villa and is now an archaeological museum displaying a variety of Roman artifacts. The house itself features mosaics, statues, and pottery that offer insight into the lifestyle and culture of the island during Roman rule. The Domus Romana is open daily from 9:00 AM to 5:00 PM, and the entrance fee is €5 for adults, with reduced prices for students and children. It's a fascinating spot for history buffs, as the villa's preservation allows visitors to walk through a Roman home as it might have appeared over 2,000 years ago.

Not far from here, the Malta National Community Art Museum is a hidden gem tucked away on St. Agatha's Street. This space showcases the contemporary and traditional works of local Maltese artists, offering an ever-changing collection that reflects the island's creative landscape. From modern paintings to photography and sculpture, the museum highlights the evolving trends in Maltese art while keeping ties to the island's traditional influences. Open daily from 10:00 AM to 6:00 PM, the museum charges a small fee of €3 for entry. The intimate setting of the museum makes it a pleasant and quiet stop for anyone wanting to explore the work of local talent.

Another highlight in Rabat is the St. Paul's Catacombs, located on St. Agatha Street. These early Christian burial sites not only offer a unique historical perspective but also double as an intriguing museum. The catacombs are spread over several levels, with some sections having been used as burial chambers as far back as the 3rd century AD. The museum aspect focuses on the fascinating practices of early Christians in Malta and the significance of these underground tombs. Visitors can explore the catacombs daily from 9:00 AM to 5:00 PM, with an entrance fee of €5 for adults and €3 for children. This site provides an eerie yet educational experience that transports you to the heart of early Christian history on the island.

Marsaxlokk

The Marsaxlokk Open Air Museum is an enriching place to discover Malta's maritime heritage, located in the heart of this charming fishing village. Set along the picturesque waterfront of Marsaxlokk Bay, the museum offers visitors an opportunity to learn about the island's long-standing relationship with the sea. The museum's collection is dedicated to Malta's traditional fishing methods, with exhibits that showcase everything from old fishing boats (including the iconic brightly painted "luzzus") to fishing tools, nets, and even some old photographs of the village's fishing community. It's a great place to start exploring Marsaxlokk, as it provides context to the local culture and traditions. Open daily from 10:00 AM to 5:00 PM, the entry fee is modest, typically around €3 for adults and free for children.

Another cultural gem in Marsaxlokk is the Parish Museum, which is housed in a small but significant building right next to the main church of St. Joseph. The museum houses a fascinating collection of religious and historical artifacts, including church furnishings, paintings, and sculptures that reflect the village's deep connection with Christianity. The museum offers a quiet and serene experience, where visitors can admire the craftsmanship of Maltese artisans and learn about the village's history and traditions. It's open from 9:00 AM to 12:00 PM and again from 3:00 PM to 6:00 PM, and there's no entry fee, though donations are encouraged.

For those keen to explore the local art scene, the Marsaxlokk Art Gallery offers a glimpse into the work of contemporary Maltese artists. Located along the picturesque waterfront, the gallery features a rotating selection of local art that often reflects themes of the sea, fishing, and Maltese life. It's a small but inviting space where visitors can enjoy paintings, sculptures, and photography that capture the essence of the island. The gallery is open daily from 11:00 AM to 6:00 PM, with free entry, making it a great stop during a leisurely walk along the bay.

Mellieha

Mellieha offers a unique mix of historical and cultural experiences, with a selection of museums and galleries that provide insight into Malta's rich past. One of the standout attractions in this village is the Mellieha Heritage Museum, located on Main Street. Housed in a traditional Maltese building, the museum offers a fascinating collection of artifacts that highlight Mellieha's history, from prehistoric times through to World War II. The displays include ancient pottery, tools, and photographs, alongside items related to the village's role in Malta's defense during wartime. The museum is open every day from 9:00 AM to 5:00 PM, with an entry fee of €5 for adults and €3 for children. A visit here offers a great overview of Mellieha's rich cultural heritage and its historical significance to the island.

For those interested in a more spiritual and artistic experience, the Church of the Assumption of Our Lady in Mellieha also offers a small museum on its premises. The museum focuses on religious artifacts, showcasing intricately designed statues, liturgical items, and paintings that represent the island's Catholic heritage. The church is a stunning example of Maltese Baroque architecture, and the museum's collection gives visitors an opportunity to delve deeper into the religious history of Mellieha and its surrounding area. The museum is open from 9:00 AM to 12:00 PM and 4:00 PM to 6:00 PM daily, and entry is free, although donations are welcomed.

For art lovers, the Mellieha Arts Centre offers a refreshing experience, with local Maltese artists frequently displaying their work in the gallery. The center hosts a variety of exhibitions, including paintings, sculptures, and multimedia art that reflect the creativity and vision of Maltese artists. The exhibitions often explore themes of nature, culture, and the island's maritime history. Located near the center of Mellieha, the Arts Centre is open daily from 10:00 AM to 7:00 PM, with free entry. It's a great place to experience the vibrant local art scene and discover the talents of Malta's contemporary artists.

Qormi

In Qormi, Malta's largest inland town, visitors can step back in time and experience the island's rich history and culture through its local museums and galleries. One of the must-visit spots is the Qormi Local Council Heritage Museum, located on Triq San Ġużepp. This small but charming museum offers a fascinating look into the town's past, with a collection that includes traditional tools, old photographs, and artifacts that tell the story of Qormi's agricultural and industrial heritage. The museum is open from Monday to Saturday, 9:00 AM to 1:00 PM, and entry is free, though donations are encouraged. It's a perfect spot for those who want to learn about the town's history in a quiet, unhurried setting.

Another gem in Qormi is the Malta Baking Museum, which focuses on the island's long tradition of bread-making, a craft that has been central to Malta's culinary heritage for centuries. Located in an old bakery, this museum showcases traditional tools used by Maltese bakers, as well as displays on the history of bread production in the area. The museum also often hosts live demonstrations, offering visitors the chance to see how traditional Maltese bread is made. Open Monday to Friday from 9:00 AM to 4:00 PM, with entry typically costing around €4 for adults and €2 for children, this museum is an immersive experience into Malta's food culture.

If you're interested in more artistic endeavors, the nearby galleries in Qormi feature the work of local Maltese artists, many of whom are inspired by the town's history and surroundings. One notable gallery in the area is the Qormi Art Centre, which showcases a mix of contemporary and traditional works, often focusing on themes of Maltese identity and local traditions. The center also runs workshops for those interested in pursuing their own creative talents. The gallery is open from 10:00 AM to 6:00 PM daily, with free entry to the exhibits.

Birkirkara

In Birkirkara, one of Malta's largest and most historically rich towns, there's plenty to explore for those interested in its past and local culture. The Birkirkara Local Council Heritage Museum, located in the heart of the town, is the perfect starting point for understanding the town's history. Housed in an old building, the museum provides a detailed look into the history of Birkirkara, with a collection of artifacts that span centuries. Visitors can view photographs, old maps, and items from various periods, showcasing the evolution of the town from its rural beginnings to its more modern developments. The museum is open from Monday to Friday, 9:00 AM to 1:00 PM, and it's free to visit, with donations appreciated. It's a great spot to learn about the local history in a relaxed setting.

For those with a particular interest in religious art, the St. Helen's Basilica Museum offers an impressive collection of ecclesiastical artifacts. Located within the Basilica itself on Triq il-Parroċċa, this museum is home to a variety of religious items, including ornate vestments, silverware, and other treasures that reflect the deep religious heritage of Birkirkara. The museum also provides a glimpse into the history of the church and the town's religious customs. Visitors can explore the museum from 9:00 AM to 12:00 PM and 3:00 PM to 6:00 PM daily. Entry is free, though donations are welcomed.

Birkirkara also has a small but vibrant art scene, and the Birkirkara Art Gallery provides an excellent venue to experience local artistic expression. The gallery often hosts exhibitions that feature the work of contemporary Maltese artists, focusing on everything from modern abstract works to more traditional forms of painting and sculpture. It's a great place to discover the talents of the island's artists, with pieces often inspired by Maltese landscapes, culture, and daily life. The gallery is open from 10:00 AM to 7:00 PM daily, and entry is free.

Birgu

In Birgu (Vittoriosa), one of the three historic cities that make up the Three Cities in Malta, visitors can step into a living history where the past is preserved and celebrated. A key stop for history enthusiasts is the Inquisitor's Palace, located on Triq il-Provveditur. This grand building, once the residence of the Inquisitor of Malta, offers a deep dive into the island's ecclesiastical and judicial past. The palace showcases a variety of exhibits, from religious artifacts to historical exhibits detailing the role of the Inquisition in Malta. The building itself, with its charming courtyard and ornate architecture, is a beautiful backdrop to the exhibits. The Inquisitor's Palace is open daily from 9:00 AM to 5:00 PM, with an entry fee of €6 for adults and €3 for children and seniors. The museum provides a fascinating glimpse into Malta's darker past while offering a peaceful setting to explore.

Not far from the Inquisitor's Palace, the Malta Maritime Museum on the Vittoriosa Waterfront offers a comprehensive exploration of Malta's maritime history. Set within a former naval bakery, this museum boasts a collection that spans from the Phoenician period to modern times, with displays of ship models, maritime tools, and naval uniforms. There are exhibits dedicated to the Order of St. John, the role of Malta during the British Empire, and even Malta's modern maritime industry. The museum is a great stop for anyone interested in the island's seafaring traditions. It's open daily from 9:00 AM to 5:00 PM, with an entry fee of €5 for adults and €3 for children.

The Birgu (Vittoriosa) area also hosts the Church of St. Lawrence, a striking example of Baroque architecture, which houses the St. Lawrence Museum. This small museum is dedicated to the life of the church's patron saint and offers religious artifacts and paintings that tell the story of St. Lawrence's role in the local community. Visitors can explore the museum and the beautiful church daily from 8:00 AM to 12:00 PM and 4:00 PM to 7:00 PM. Entrance is free, though donations are encouraged.

For those looking for something more contemporary, the Birgu Arts and Crafts Gallery is a wonderful spot to experience the work of local Maltese artists. Located near the waterfront, this small gallery features a rotating collection of artwork, including paintings, photography, and sculptures that reflect both the local landscape and the vibrant culture of Malta. The gallery is open from 10:00 AM to 6:00 PM daily, and entry is free, making it an accessible stop during a day of exploration in Birgu.

Senglea

Senglea, or Isla, is one of the three cities that form the historic heart of Malta, and it offers visitors a unique glimpse into the island's rich past. The town's small size doesn't detract from the depth of history and culture it holds, particularly through its museums and galleries, each reflecting a different aspect of the island's heritage.

One of the standout spots in Senglea is the Gardjola Gardens, which, while not a traditional museum, offers stunning views and a bit of local history. Situated at the tip of the Senglea peninsula, this garden is a peaceful retreat, complete with historical inscriptions and a beautiful watchtower. The Gardjola tower was originally used for military purposes and, in the gardens, visitors can learn about the fortifications that once guarded the entrance to the Grand Harbour. While there's no entry fee, it's open daily from 8:00 AM to 6:00 PM, and it's an excellent spot to reflect on the area's strategic significance.

For a deeper dive into Senglea's maritime history, the Maritime Museum of Senglea offers a more intimate experience. Located along the waterfront, this smaller museum is often overlooked but provides a detailed look at the role Senglea played in Malta's naval defense. The exhibits focus on the town's seafaring past, especially its involvement in the Great Siege of 1565. The museum houses a collection of naval artifacts, including ship models, weaponry, and historical documents. It's open Tuesday to Saturday from 10:00 AM to 5:00 PM, and entry is priced at €4 for adults, with reduced rates for children and seniors. The museum's location by the sea makes it a pleasant visit, with the salty breeze adding to the maritime atmosphere.

Another must-visit is the Church of Our Lady of Victories, a site of great historical importance in Senglea. Although the church itself is a stunning Baroque structure, it also features a small museum dedicated to the Order of St. John and their contributions to Malta's defense, especially during the Great Siege. The church is open every day from 9:00 AM to 12:00 PM and from 4:00 PM to 7:00 PM, and entry is free, though donations are encouraged. The museum inside the church gives visitors a deeper understanding of the town's strategic importance during the era of the Knights of St. John.

The area around Senglea is also home to several small galleries that showcase the work of contemporary Maltese artists. The Senglea Art Gallery, located near the town center, regularly exhibits paintings, sculptures, and photography from local artists. These works often reflect the beauty of Senglea itself and its surroundings, capturing the essence of the three cities and the Mediterranean lifestyle. The gallery is open daily from 10:00 AM to 6:00 PM, with free entry, making it an accessible stop for anyone interested in the current Maltese art scene.

Cospicua

Cospicua, or Bormla, one of the Three Cities, is a town steeped in rich history and offers a selection of museums and galleries that showcase Malta's maritime and cultural heritage. The town, once a significant naval stronghold, provides visitors with a deeper understanding of the island's storied past.

The Malta Maritime Museum, located in the heart of Cospicua at the historic Naval Bakery, is the key cultural institution in the area. The museum offers a thorough exploration of Malta's seafaring history, with exhibits covering everything from the

Knights of St. John and their naval operations to Malta's role during World War II. Inside, visitors can explore an impressive collection of ship models, ancient maritime tools, and naval uniforms. The museum also houses a fascinating selection of documents and photographs that illustrate Malta's long-standing connection to the sea. The Malta Maritime Museum is open daily from 9:00 AM to 5:00 PM, with an entry fee of €5 for adults and €3 for children and seniors. The museum's waterfront location allows visitors to take in the beauty of the Grand Harbour after exploring the exhibits.

Another must-see in Cospicua is the Inquisitor's Palace, located in the heart of the town. This historic building, which once served as the residence of the Inquisitor of Malta, now houses a museum dedicated to the history of the Inquisition and the church's judicial influence in Malta. The palace is an impressive example of Baroque architecture, and its collections reflect both religious and legal aspects of Malta's past. Visitors can explore the palace's grand rooms and learn about the role of the Inquisition in Malta's history, as well as the various ecclesiastical practices of the time. The Inquisitor's Palace is open daily from 9:00 AM to 5:00 PM, with an entry fee of €6 for adults and €3 for children and seniors.

For art lovers, the Cospicua Art Gallery offers a chance to discover the work of local Maltese artists. Located near the town's central square, this small but vibrant gallery features contemporary works, including paintings, sculptures, and photography. The gallery's exhibitions often reflect the themes of Maltese culture, with many pieces inspired by the island's landscapes, architecture, and daily life. The gallery is open from 10:00 AM to 6:00 PM daily, and entry is free, making it an accessible spot to enjoy and purchase art from local creators.

In addition to these highlights, Cospicua is home to several historical buildings and churches that add to the town's cultural landscape. St. Lawrence Church, for example, is an excellent example of Baroque architecture and features stunning artwork that reflects the town's rich religious history. While not a traditional museum, the church is a significant historical site in the area and offers insight into the spiritual life of Cospicua.

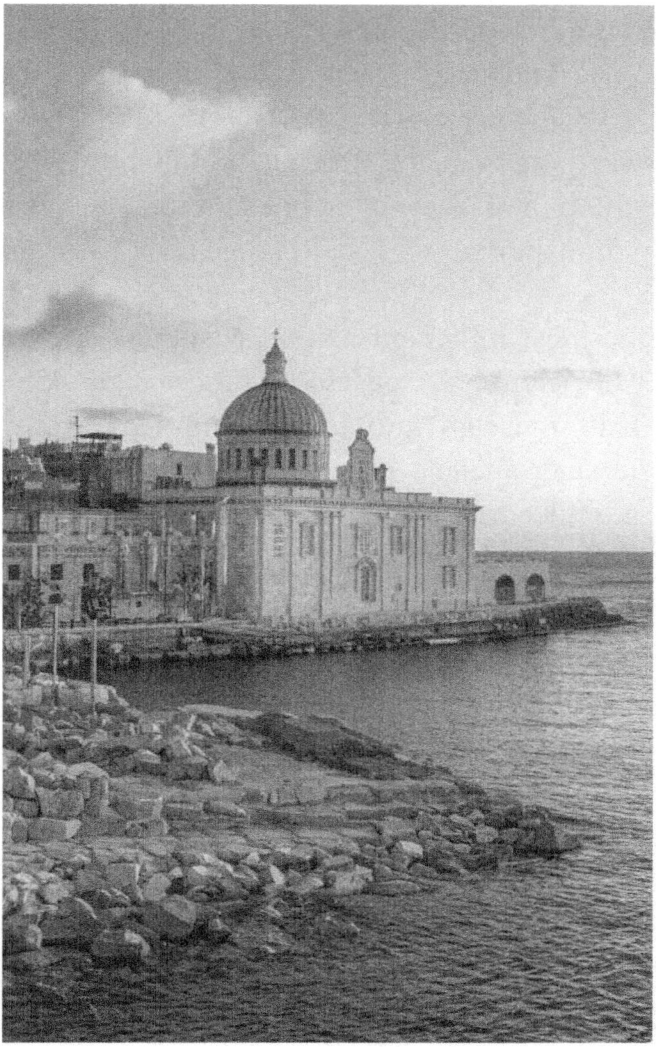

Gozo

Victoria

Victoria, also known as Rabat, is the capital of Gozo and is home to several museums and galleries that reflect the island's rich history and vibrant artistic community. The town's narrow streets and ancient architecture provide the perfect backdrop for exploring these cultural gems.

One of the most important historical sites in Victoria is the National Museum of Archaeology, located at 43 Republic Street. This museum provides an in-depth look at the prehistoric and ancient history of Gozo and Malta. The museum's collection spans thousands of years, featuring artifacts from the island's Neolithic period, including tools, pottery, and statues, along with the famous Venus of Malta. The museum offers a fascinating journey through Malta's earliest civilizations, highlighting its role as a key Mediterranean hub in ancient times. It is open daily from 9:00 AM to 5:00 PM, with an entry fee of €6 for adults and €3 for children, students, and seniors.

For those interested in a more in-depth historical experience, the Cittadella Visitor Centre is a must-visit. Located within the historic Cittadella fortress, the Visitor Centre provides a detailed exhibition on the history of the Citadel and the surrounding area. The Citadel, a fortified hilltop settlement, offers panoramic views of Gozo and is one of the most significant landmarks on the island. The Visitor Centre presents the Citadel's past, from its role in ancient defense to its strategic importance throughout Malta's history. The center is open daily from 9:00 AM to 5:00 PM, with an entry fee of €5 for adults and €2 for children and seniors.

While in the Citadel, visitors should also check out the Cittadella Museum, located in the former Bishop's Palace. This museum presents a fascinating array of artifacts that tell the story of Gozo's social and religious history, with displays on the island's traditional crafts, art, and the influence of various civilizations over the centuries. The museum is open from 9:00 AM to 5:00 PM, with a fee of €5 for adults and discounted rates for children and seniors.

For a more artistic experience, the Gozo Art Gallery, located near Republic Street, offers a showcase of contemporary local art. The gallery exhibits paintings, sculptures, and mixed-media works by Maltese and Gozo-based artists. It's an excellent place to discover the artistic scene on Gozo, with many works inspired by the island's landscapes, culture, and history. The gallery is open daily from 10:00 AM to 6:00 PM, and entry is free, making it an accessible stop for art lovers.

Additionally, visitors can explore the Ta' Kola Windmill, which is not only a historical site but also a small museum where you can learn about the island's agricultural past and the importance of windmills in Gozo's history. The museum offers a unique look at the tools and techniques used in grain milling and is a great way to understand the island's rural traditions. It's open daily from 9:00 AM to 5:00 PM, with an entry fee of €3 for adults and €2 for children.

Xlendi

Xlendi, a charming coastal village on the island of Gozo, may be small, but it offers a tranquil setting for those looking to explore the island's history and art scene. While the village is primarily known for its stunning bay and crystal-clear waters, it also boasts a few gems for history buffs and art lovers.

One of the most notable cultural sites in Xlendi is the Xlendi Tower, a historic watchtower that dates back to the 17th century. While it's not a traditional museum, the tower offers insight into Malta's defense systems during the time of the Knights of St. John. The tower was strategically placed to keep watch over the bay and its surroundings, and today it provides an excellent view of the coastline and the Mediterranean Sea. Visitors can explore the tower and enjoy the panoramic views, but it is generally open by appointment or during special events. There is no fixed entry fee, though donations are encouraged to help preserve the site.

While Xlendi may not have a wealth of traditional museums, the surrounding area has several small galleries that showcase local art. The Gozo Art Gallery, located a short distance from Xlendi, is a must-see for anyone interested in contemporary Maltese art. The gallery often features the work of local Gozo-based artists, offering a collection of paintings, sculptures, and mixed-media works. The pieces on display often reflect the beauty of Gozo's landscapes and the island's cultural traditions. The gallery is open daily from 10:00 AM to 6:00 PM, with free entry, making it an accessible stop for art lovers.

For those who enjoy outdoor art, the surrounding cliffs of Xlendi offer opportunities to appreciate nature's beauty in its purest form. Walking along the cliffs, you can enjoy the peaceful landscape, which has inspired many local artists. While there are no formal art installations along the cliffs, the natural setting itself serves as an ever-changing canvas, with each season bringing new colors and textures to the landscape.

Xlendi also hosts a few small artisan shops where local craftsmen showcase their work. Visitors can find handmade pottery, jewelry, and paintings inspired by the island's natural beauty. These small, local shops offer a great opportunity to take home a unique piece of Gozo's culture and artistry.

Marsalforn

Marsalforn, a vibrant seaside village in Gozo, may be best known for its beautiful bay and bustling promenade, but it also offers visitors a chance to explore the island's cultural history through its small yet charming museums and galleries.

One of the most interesting stops in Marsalforn is the Ggantija Temples, located just a short distance from the village. While the site is not in Marsalforn itself, it is close enough to make it a worthwhile visit. These ancient temples, which date back to 3600 BC, are a UNESCO World Heritage site and provide a fascinating look at Malta's prehistoric past. The temples are one of the oldest freestanding structures in the world, and the visitor center offers educational displays on the history and significance of the site. Open daily from 9:00 AM to 5:00 PM, with an entry fee of €10 for adults and €5 for children, it's an essential stop for history enthusiasts.

For a more contemporary art experience, the Gozo Art Gallery, located near the heart of Marsalforn, offers a selection of local and international works. The gallery showcases the creative output of Gozo-based artists, with exhibitions that include a mix of paintings, sculptures, and photography. The vibrant pieces often reflect the island's unique landscapes, traditions, and coastal beauty. The gallery is open daily from 10:00 AM to 6:00 PM, and entry is free, making it a great stop for those wanting to immerse themselves in Gozo's artistic community.

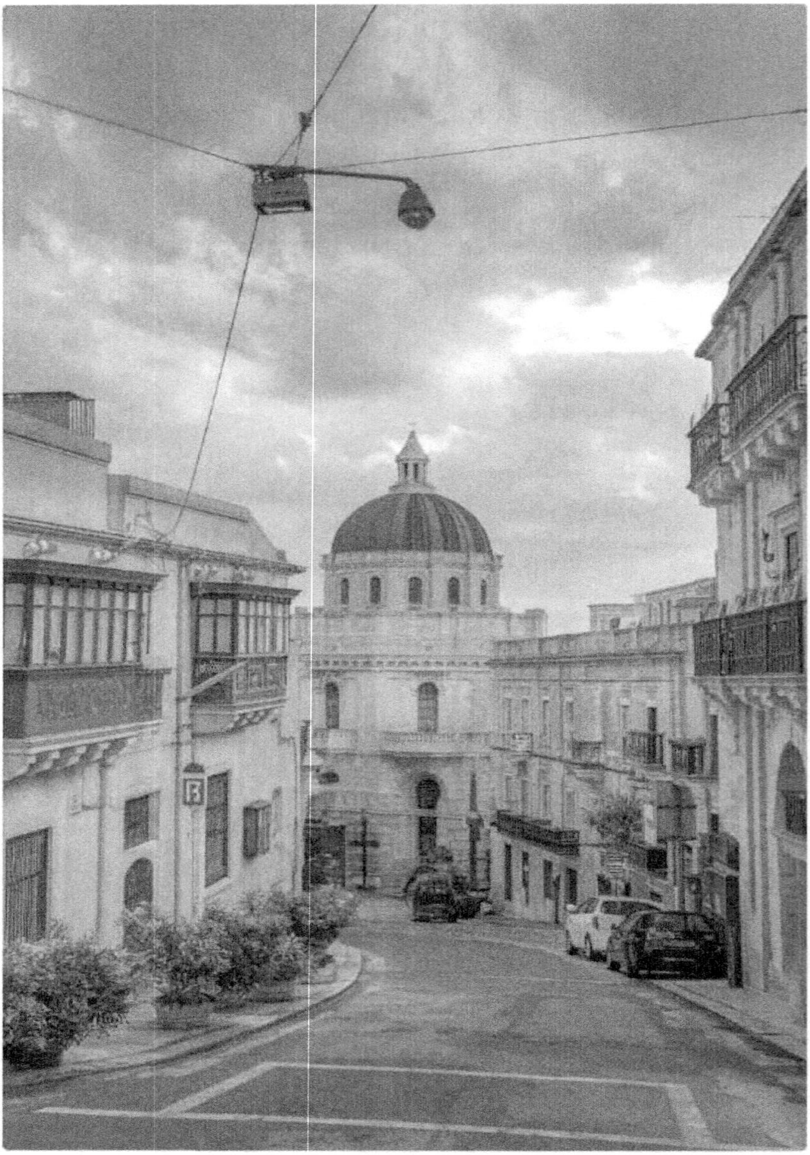

Historical & Cultural Gems

Ancient Temples and Sites

In Gozo, the Ġgantija Temples are a standout attraction for anyone interested in the island's ancient history. Located near Xagħra, just a short distance from Marsalforn, these temples are among the oldest freestanding structures in the world, with their origins dating back to around 3600 BC. The site is a remarkable testament to Malta's prehistoric inhabitants, and standing among the massive stone walls offers an almost surreal experience. The temples are older than the pyramids of Egypt, making them a unique window into the island's ancient past.

The layout of the site includes two main temples, which are surrounded by an impressive wall. The grandeur of the structure is stunning, and as you wander around, it's easy to marvel at the ingenuity of those who built it. The visitor center provides context, showcasing the artifacts discovered on-site, including pottery and tools, which paint a clearer picture of how the temples were used in religious practices.

While Ġgantija is the most well-known, another interesting site in Gozo is the Ta' Kola Windmill. Situated in Xagħra as well, it offers a peek into the island's agricultural past.

Though not as ancient, this windmill dates back to the 17th century and stands as a symbol of Gozo's rural traditions. It is remarkably well-preserved, and inside, visitors can learn about the miller's life and how grain was ground, all while taking in sweeping views of the surrounding countryside.

For anyone interested in more ancient landmarks, the Cittadella in Victoria is a must-see. It's an ancient fortified city that dates back to the Phoenician period, and its strategic location atop a hill offers spectacular views of the island. Within the walls of the Cittadella, visitors can walk through narrow streets, discover old bastions, and take in the history of this fortified town, which served as the island's center of power and defense over centuries.

UNESCO World Heritage Sites

Gozo is home to one of Malta's most iconic UNESCO World Heritage Sites, the Ġgantija Temples. These ancient megalithic structures, dating back to around 3600 BC, are among the oldest freestanding buildings in the world. Situated in Xagħra, just a short drive from Marsalforn, the site is both awe-inspiring and humbling. Walking among the towering stones, it's easy to appreciate how skilled the early Maltese people were to have created such structures with limited tools, using massive limestone blocks that still stand firm today.

The Ġgantija Temples consist of two main temples, surrounded by an impressive wall. While much of the site has been restored, you can still feel the connection to the past as you walk through the ruins, imagining the rituals and ceremonies that took place here thousands of years ago. A visitor center at the site provides additional context, displaying artifacts like pottery and tools found during excavations. These finds offer a glimpse into the daily lives of the people who once inhabited this extraordinary site.

Not far from Ġgantija, the Cittadella in Victoria is another important historical site and a symbol of Gozo's rich cultural history. This ancient citadel was once the island's hub for defense and governance, dating back to the Phoenician period. Its commanding position atop a hill offers sweeping views of the island, making it an ideal spot to appreciate Gozo's natural beauty and strategic importance throughout history. The Cittadella is home to a collection of museums and churches that detail its role in Gozo's defense and daily life over the centuries. Walking through its narrow streets and fortified walls gives a unique sense of the island's medieval and Renaissance past.

Fortresses and Citadels

Gozo's landscape is shaped by history, and few sites capture that more vividly than the Cittadella in Victoria. Sitting atop a hill, this impressive fortress dominates the skyline, offering both a glimpse into the island's past and stunning views of the surrounding countryside. The Cittadella has stood the test of time, with its origins dating back to the Phoenician period, though much of what we see today was built during the medieval era. It served as Gozo's central defense hub, offering protection against invaders over the centuries.

Walking through the Cittadella is like stepping back in time. The stone walls, narrow passages, and old cannons evoke a sense of what life was like during the turbulent periods of Malta's history. The site houses several museums, including the Gozo Archaeological Museum, which showcases artifacts from the island's long history, and the Museum of the History of the Cittadella, which walks visitors through its military and cultural significance. From the top, the panoramic view of Gozo is nothing short of spectacular, allowing you to appreciate how strategically important the site was for centuries. The entrance to the Cittadella is free, though donations are welcome, and it's open every day from 9:00 AM to 5:00 PM.

A short distance from the Cittadella, you'll find the Ta' Xbiex Battery, another important fortress on the island, offering a quieter experience. Originally built during the British period, this smaller fortification was strategically placed to defend the entrance to the harbor. Though not as well-known as the Cittadella, it's an interesting place to visit for those wanting to see how Malta's military history has evolved over the centuries.

Museums and Art Galleries

Marsalforn, though a charming seaside village, offers visitors a few cultural spots that provide a deep dive into Gozo's heritage, both ancient and contemporary.

One of the standout attractions in the area is the nearby Ġgantija Temples, located just a short drive from Marsalforn. While not technically in the village, these temples are an essential stop for those interested in the island's ancient history. Dating back to around 3600 BC, Ġgantija is one of the world's oldest freestanding stone structures. The site is part of a UNESCO World Heritage collection and offers an immersive experience, complete with a visitor center that explains the significance of the temples and their construction. It is open daily from 9:00 AM to 5:00 PM, with an entry fee of €10 for adults and €5 for children. The site provides visitors with a fascinating glimpse into Malta's prehistoric past and is a must-see when in the area.

In Marsalforn itself, the Gozo Art Gallery is one of the key venues to explore the island's vibrant local art scene. Located near the center of the village, this gallery showcases a rotating selection of works from Maltese and Gozo-based artists, including paintings, photography, and sculptures. The gallery is a great place to discover the talents of local artists, many of whom draw inspiration from the island's natural beauty and cultural history. The Gozo Art Gallery is open daily from 10:00 AM to 6:00 PM, and entry is free, making it an accessible and worthwhile stop for art enthusiasts.

For visitors looking for a more intimate and traditional view of local life, the nearby Għarb Folklore Museum, while not directly in Marsalforn, is just a short drive away and offers a unique collection of Gozo's cultural history. The museum showcases traditional Maltese artifacts, including clothing, tools, and household items that reflect the daily lives of past generations. The museum is open daily from 9:00 AM to 5:00 PM, with an entry fee of €4 for adults and €2 for children. It offers a fascinating look at Gozo's cultural heritage and is perfect for those who want to understand the island's local traditions and customs.

Festivals and Local Events

Gozo's festivals and local events offer an authentic and vibrant look into the island's culture, traditions, and the lively spirit of its people. Throughout the year, visitors can enjoy a range of experiences, from religious celebrations to artistic showcases, each reflecting the island's unique blend of history and modernity.

One of the most significant events on Gozo's calendar is the Feast of St. George in Victoria. This annual celebration, held in late April or early May, draws thousands of locals and visitors alike. The streets of Victoria come alive with colorful processions, music, and fireworks. The feast is a blend of religious devotion and festive celebration, with a procession carrying the statue of St. George through the streets, accompanied by traditional bands and the sound of fireworks echoing across the island. The atmosphere is lively, filled with the smell of street food and the sounds of the crowds, making it an essential experience for anyone visiting Gozo during this time.

In the summer months, the Carnival of Gozo brings a burst of color and excitement to the island. Celebrated in February or March, just before Lent, the carnival is a lively spectacle filled with flamboyant costumes, parades, and street parties. While the festivities in Victoria are the largest, smaller villages also host their own events, each with unique traditions and local flair. The carnival is a time of joy, with locals coming together to celebrate before the more solemn days of Lent, and visitors can expect to see a range of activities, from costume contests to performances in the streets.

For those interested in arts and culture, the annual Gozo International Arts Festival is a must-attend event. Held in various locations across the island, this festival showcases the best of Gozo's creative scene, from contemporary art exhibitions to theater performances and live music. The festival typically takes place in the fall, and it's an opportunity for local and international artists to present their work to a wider audience. The relaxed atmosphere of the island combined with the festival's artistic offerings makes it a perfect occasion for anyone with an appreciation for culture.

Gozo also celebrates the harvest season with the Feast of the Assumption in August, one of the biggest religious events of the year. The feast is held in several villages, but it is particularly grand in Xagħra, where the streets are decorated, and there are processions, fireworks, and celebrations that continue late into the night. The island's agricultural roots are honored with local produce on display, and visitors can taste traditional Gozitan foods and delicacies.

In the cooler months, the Christmas and New Year period brings with it a series of smaller but equally charming events. Villages across Gozo decorate their streets with festive lights, and local churches hold midnight Masses and nativity displays. While quieter than the summer festivals, the Christmas celebrations are a warm and welcoming time to experience Gozo's community spirit.

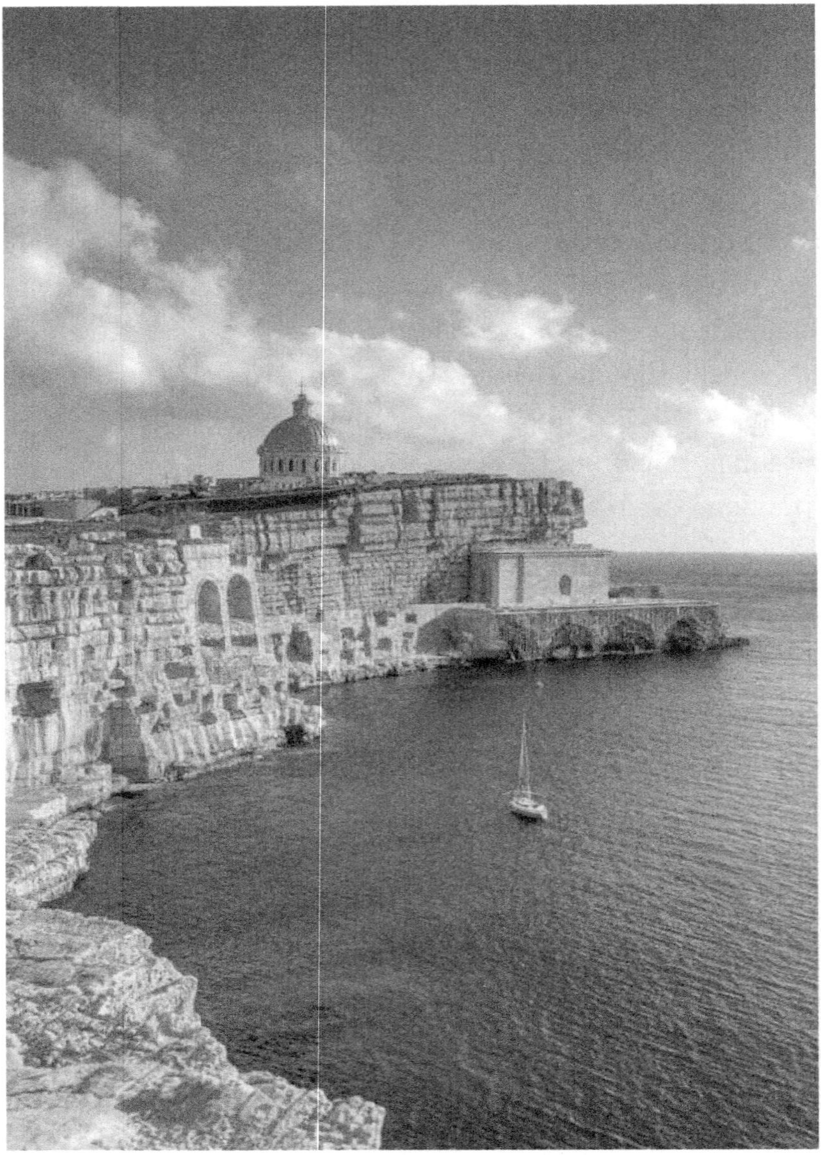

Outdoor Adventures

National Parks and Reserves

Gozo offers a variety of natural landscapes that have been preserved through national parks and reserves, giving visitors the chance to experience the island's untouched beauty while protecting its unique ecosystems. These natural areas are perfect for those who enjoy outdoor exploration, whether it's a peaceful walk through scenic trails or a more adventurous hike with breathtaking views.

One of the most notable natural sites is the Ta' Cenc Cliffs, a protected area offering panoramic views over the Mediterranean Sea. Located at the southern edge of Gozo, the cliffs are known for their dramatic beauty and rich biodiversity. Visitors can take leisurely walks along the cliffside paths, enjoying the stunning views of the sea below and the rugged coastline. The area is home to several species of Mediterranean plants and birds, making it a haven for nature lovers and birdwatchers. While there are no entrance fees, visitors are encouraged to respect the natural environment and follow the marked trails to avoid disturbing the local wildlife.

Another beautiful natural area is the Ramla Bay Nature Reserve, located on the north coast of Gozo. This sandy beach, with its distinctive red sands, is one of the island's most popular natural attractions. The reserve is not only a beautiful spot for sunbathing and swimming but also offers a chance to explore its surrounding hills, which are home to various plant and animal species. The reserve is a crucial nesting site for sea turtles, making it a significant location for conservation efforts. Ramla Bay is free to visit and open year-round, with the best time to visit being during the spring and autumn months when the weather is ideal for outdoor activities.

Gozo's Inland Sea, another stunning natural feature, is a lagoon formed within a limestone cave, surrounded by cliffs that rise steeply from the water. The Inland Sea is part of the Dwejra Bay, which is protected as a nature reserve. The area is known for its natural rock formations, and visitors can take boat trips through the tunnel that connects the inland sea to the open Mediterranean. It's a great spot for diving and exploring the underwater world. While the site is open to the public year-round, boat trips are usually offered between April and October, and entry is free.

The Xwejni Salt Pans, located on the northwestern coast of Gozo, are a testament to the island's agricultural heritage. L

Hiking and Walking Trails

Gozo is a paradise for those who enjoy hiking and walking, with a network of trails that offer spectacular views of the island's rugged coastline, rolling hills, and tranquil landscapes. Whether you're looking for a short stroll or a more challenging hike, Gozo's walking trails cater to all levels of experience.

One of the most popular trails on Gozo is the walk along the Xlendi to the Salt Pans. This relatively easy trail starts at the picturesque Xlendi Bay, where you can take in the view of the clear blue waters before heading inland toward the famous Xwejni Salt Pans. The route offers fantastic coastal views, passing through fields and along cliffs. It's a great way to experience the island's natural beauty while learning about Gozo's long tradition of salt production. The trail is well-marked and takes about 1.5 to 2 hours, depending on your pace. The best time to tackle this walk is in the cooler months, as the summer heat can make it more challenging.

For those looking for something a bit more challenging, the walk from the Cittadella to Ta' Cenc Cliffs offers stunning vistas of Gozo and the surrounding islands. The trail begins at the Cittadella, the fortified citadel in Victoria, and heads south through farmland and rocky terrain. As you make your way along the cliffs, the views of the Mediterranean Sea and Malta's coastline are simply breathtaking. The walk is moderate to strenuous, and can take up to 3 hours, but the reward is worth it. The Ta' Cenc Cliffs are a haven for birdwatchers, with a variety of species making their homes here. This trail is especially beautiful during spring when the island is in full bloom.

The Gozo Coastal Walk, which runs along the entire coastline of Gozo, is a long-distance trail that offers some of the most stunning views on the island. The trail is split into sections, each of which showcases a different part of Gozo's coastline. From the southern shores near the Ta' Cenc Cliffs to the northern beaches like Ramla Bay, this trail takes you through a variety of landscapes, including cliffs, valleys, and sandy shores. It's a more demanding trail, requiring several days to complete, but it offers a truly immersive experience of Gozo's natural beauty. For shorter walks, sections of the trail can be enjoyed individually, with the option to take public transport back to the starting point.

For a unique experience, the walk to the Dwejra Bay is a must. This area is home to the famous Inland Sea and the natural rock formation known as the Azure Window, which collapsed in 2017 but still remains a stunning part of Gozo's landscape. The walk to Dwejra Bay is not too difficult and can be completed in about an hour. You'll pass through fields, coastal paths, and get a chance to see Gozo's rich flora and fauna. The Inland Sea itself is a highlight, with the option to take a boat ride through the natural tunnel that connects it to the open sea. The views here are magnificent, especially at sunset when the light casts a golden glow over the water and cliffs.

Another charming walk can be found at the Wied il-Mielah, a hidden valley near the village of Gharb. This picturesque walk takes you through a peaceful valley and along the coastline, passing by the unique Wied il-Mielah Window, a natural limestone arch. The walk offers spectacular views of the sea and surrounding countryside, with relatively little foot traffic, making it a great option for those seeking a quieter, more serene experience. The trail is about 1.5 hours long and is suitable for all levels.

Water Sports and Beach Activities

Malta and Gozo are all about the sea. With their clear waters, rocky coves, and sandy beaches, they offer some of the best spots in the Mediterranean for water sports and beach activities. Whether you're looking to take it slow with a peaceful paddle along the coast or dive straight into high-energy action, the islands have plenty to offer.

For those who love the adrenaline rush of speed and waves, jet skiing is one of the most popular activities, especially around Golden Bay, Mellieħa Bay, and St. George's Bay in Malta. Rentals are available along the beaches, and it doesn't take long to get the hang of it. In Gozo, Ramla Bay and Hondoq ir-Rummien are great places to jump on a jet ski and explore the coastline from a different perspective. If you're after something a little more social, banana boat rides and parasailing are just as fun and available at most major beach spots.

Kayaking is one of the best ways to explore the islands' hidden sea caves and remote beaches that aren't accessible by land. In Malta, the stretch between St. Peter's Pool and Marsaxlokk is a fantastic route, passing dramatic cliffs and secluded bays. In Gozo, kayaking from Xlendi Bay to Fungus Rock takes you past some of the island's most iconic coastal scenery. For a more relaxed paddle, the waters around Comino are calm and ideal for exploring at your own pace, especially around the famous Blue Lagoon and Crystal Lagoon.

If you'd rather be under the water than on top of it, snorkeling and diving in Malta and Gozo are some of the best in Europe. The Blue Hole in Gozo is one of the most famous dive spots, offering a dramatic underwater arch and deep blue visibility that feels almost surreal. Other fantastic dive sites include Inland Sea, Wied il-Għasri, and the wrecks off Ċirkewwa in Malta, where you can explore sunken ships and marine life up close. For snorkelers, Għar Lapsi and Fomm ir-Riħ offer clear, shallow waters teeming with fish, making them great spots even for beginners.

Stand-up paddleboarding has become increasingly popular in recent years, offering a peaceful yet active way to take in the coastline. Mistra Bay in Malta is a great place for first-timers, with its calm, sheltered waters, while the stretch from San Blas Bay in Gozo offers a scenic paddle past cliffs and caves. The early morning hours are the best time to get out on the water before the beaches get busy.

For something completely different, night swimming and bioluminescent snorkeling are experiences that take full advantage of Malta and Gozo's clear waters. Certain areas, like Dwejra and Comino, have waters that glow under the right conditions, giving night-time snorkeling an almost otherworldly feel. It's not an everyday activity, but some local guides run special night tours for those looking to try something out of the ordinary.

For travelers who want a mix of beach lounging and activity, Malta and Gozo have plenty of beaches where you can do both. Golden Bay and Għajn Tuffieħa in Malta are perfect for relaxing on the sand, while Hondoq ir-Rummien in Gozo has shallow, crystal-clear waters that are ideal for swimming. If you prefer a livelier scene, St. George's Bay in Malta is one of the busier beaches, with plenty of activities available.

Diving and Snorkeling Spots

Gozo is one of the Mediterranean's top diving and snorkeling destinations, with its clear waters, dramatic underwater landscapes, and abundant marine life. The island's rugged coastline hides submerged caves, tunnels, and reefs, making it an exciting place for both experienced divers and those looking to try snorkeling in a stunning natural setting.

One of the most famous dive sites is the Blue Hole at Dwejra. This natural rock formation creates a spectacular entry point for divers, leading into an underwater cavern with stunning light effects. The site, which was once located beneath the now-collapsed Azure Window, remains one of the most breathtaking dives in Gozo. Beyond the hole, divers can explore an intricate system of tunnels and swim-throughs, with marine life including barracudas, moray eels, and octopuses. The depth and currents make this dive better suited for those with some experience, but even snorkelers can enjoy the surface-level views around the rocky edges.

Nearby, the Inland Sea offers another fantastic dive site. Connected to the open sea through a narrow tunnel, this spot features a dramatic underwater passage leading to open waters. Divers love the contrast between the shallow, calm lagoon and the deeper, darker exit, where the seabed drops away into the deep blue. Snorkelers can enjoy the sheltered waters within the Inland Sea, where small fish and colorful marine plants thrive.

For those looking for an easier shore dive, Xlendi Bay is an excellent choice. The bay offers a more relaxed environment, making it ideal for beginners and snorkelers. The main attraction here is the Xlendi Tunnel, a 70-meter-long passage that starts just a few meters from the shore. The tunnel opens into a bright, open cavern with stunning blue water illuminated by sunlight. Snorkelers can stay near the entrance, where small fish and sea urchins cling to the rocks, while divers can venture deeper to explore the cave system.

On the northern coast, Reqqa Point is one of Gozo's most thrilling dive sites, known for its steep drop-offs and abundance of marine life. The vertical walls of this site are covered in coral and sponges, while schools of fish, groupers, and even the occasional tuna can be seen patrolling the deep. This dive is best suited for advanced divers due to the depth and occasional strong currents, but for those up to the challenge, it offers one of the most rewarding underwater experiences in the region.

For those who prefer snorkeling, Hondoq ir-Rummien is one of the best spots on the island. Located on the southeastern coast near Qala, this bay features crystal-clear waters and a shallow seabed filled with marine life. The rocky coastline provides plenty of small caves and crevices to explore, making it a great place to see colorful fish, starfish, and sea cucumbers. The calm waters make it perfect for families and those who want to enjoy an easy, relaxed snorkeling session.

Another excellent snorkeling location is Mgarr ix-Xini, a quiet and sheltered bay on the southern coast. The water here is clear and calm, making it ideal for spotting fish and small octopuses hiding among the rocks. The beach itself is small and peaceful, offering a great place to relax after a swim.

Wildlife and Nature Tours

Gozo's natural beauty is best experienced through its wildlife and nature tours, which offer a chance to explore the island's rugged landscapes, diverse habitats, and rich biodiversity. From birdwatching along dramatic cliffs to spotting marine life in hidden coves, the island provides plenty of opportunities for nature lovers to immerse themselves in the wild side of Malta's sister island.

One of the best ways to discover Gozo's wildlife is on a guided hike through Ta' Cenc Cliffs, where breathtaking views meet a thriving ecosystem. Rising steeply from the sea, these limestone cliffs are home to rare plants and seabirds, including the Scopoli's shearwater and the Yelkouan shearwater, which nest in the crevices. The area is a birdwatcher's paradise, particularly in the early morning or late afternoon when these seabirds glide effortlessly over the cliffs. A guided tour with a local expert can provide fascinating insight into their migratory patterns and conservation efforts.

For those interested in marine life, Dwejra Bay offers an unforgettable nature tour. The waters surrounding this bay are part of a marine conservation area, making it one of the best places to spot marine wildlife. Boat tours from the Inland Sea take visitors through a natural tunnel leading to the open sea, where you might encounter dolphins, sea turtles, and an array of colorful fish. The underwater world here is just as impressive as the rugged landscape above, and many tours include snorkeling opportunities in the crystal-clear waters.

Another must-visit spot is Wied il-Mielah, a hidden valley that offers a mix of birdwatching, wildflower spotting, and stunning rock formations. This valley is home to several species of lizards, butterflies, and native Mediterranean plants that bloom in the cooler months. Spring is the best time to visit, as the landscape comes alive with wildflowers, including orchids and rock roses, making it a dream for photographers and nature enthusiasts.

For a more interactive experience, Gozo's Eco-Farm Tours offer visitors a chance to learn about sustainable farming on the island. These tours take place at organic farms where visitors can see traditional agricultural practices in action, meet farm animals, and sample fresh produce straight from the fields. It's a great way to connect with Gozo's rural heritage while gaining a deeper appreciation for the island's environmental conservation efforts.

Gozo also offers boat-based wildlife tours, particularly around Comino's Blue Lagoon and Santa Marija Caves, where seabirds nest and marine life flourishes. These eco-friendly tours focus on responsible wildlife watching, often including stops at sea caves where you can see nesting birds, underwater caves, and even the occasional monk seal, a species that was once common in Maltese waters but is now incredibly rare.

For visitors looking to explore the island's nature at their own pace, the Gozo Coastal Walk provides an excellent self-guided alternative. Stretching around the island, this route takes in Gozo's most scenic natural spots, from dramatic cliffs and

green valleys to quiet beaches where seabirds, lizards, and wildflowers thrive.

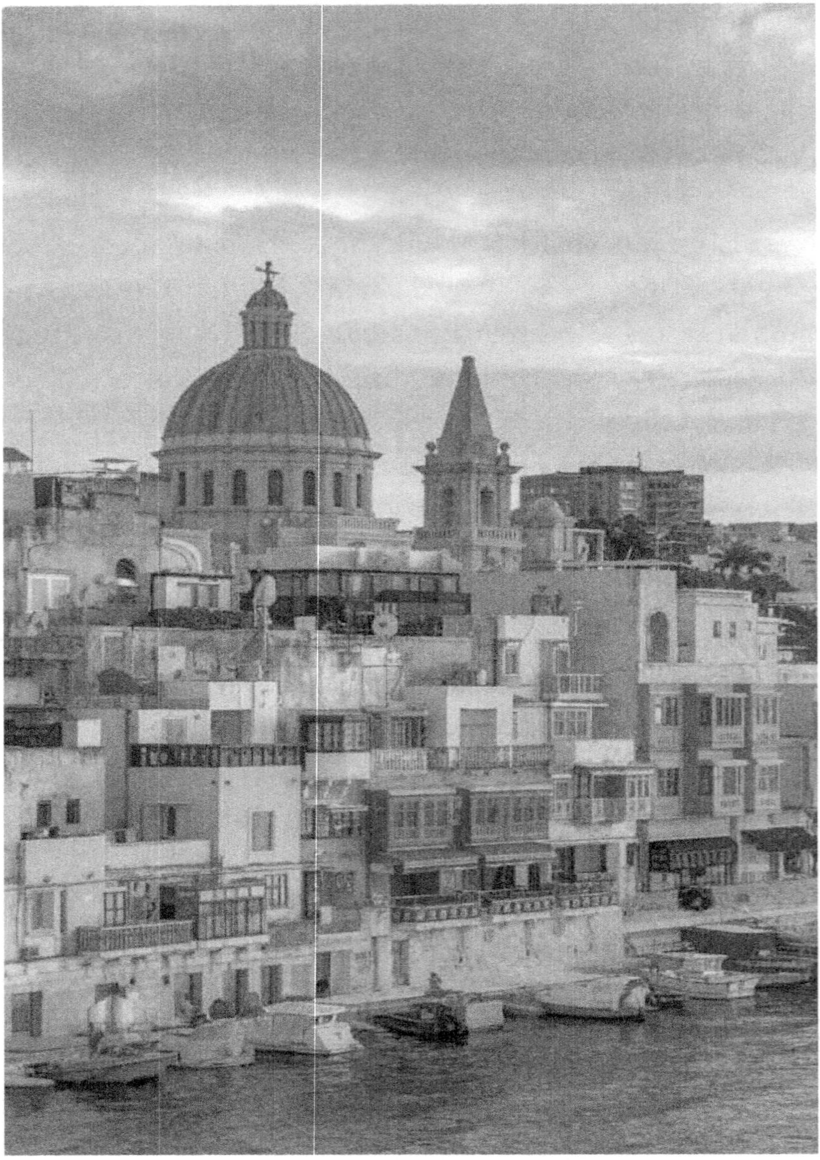

Maltese Cuisine

Must-Try Dishes and Desserts

Gozo's culinary scene is a reflection of the island's history, culture, and strong agricultural traditions. With fresh local ingredients, time-honored recipes, and Mediterranean influences, the island's must-try dishes and desserts offer an authentic taste of Gozo's identity. Whether you're dining in a traditional family-run restaurant or grabbing a snack from a village bakery, the flavors of Gozo are as rich as its landscapes.

One of the most iconic dishes is Fenek Moqli, a slow-cooked rabbit stew that is considered Malta's national dish. While it's popular across the country, Gozo's version is particularly special, often prepared with red wine, garlic, and aromatic herbs. The meat is tender and full of flavor, served with roast potatoes or crusty bread to soak up the delicious sauce. Many local restaurants in Gozo serve this dish, especially in smaller villages where recipes have been passed down for generations.

Another must-try is Gbejniet, small round cheeselets made from sheep's or goat's milk. This traditional Gozitan cheese comes in different varieties—fresh and soft, dried and aged, or peppered and marinated. The fresh version is mild and creamy, while the aged one has a more intense, slightly salty flavor. Gbejniet is often served with local honey, olives, and sundried tomatoes, or crumbled over salads and pasta dishes.

For something quick and satisfying, Ftira Għawdxija is Gozo's take on the classic Maltese ftira, a baked flatbread that's generously topped with fresh tomatoes, olives, capers, tuna, onions, and sometimes potatoes. This dish is the ultimate comfort food, with its crispy edges and rich Mediterranean flavors. It's best enjoyed at one of the local bakeries, fresh out of the oven and still warm.

Seafood lovers should try Aljotta, a traditional fish soup that is both simple and flavorful. Made with the catch of the day, usually a white fish like grouper or bream, the broth is infused with garlic, tomatoes, fresh herbs, and a hint of lemon. It's light yet satisfying, perfect as a starter before diving into a hearty main course.

Pasta dishes also play a significant role in Gozitan cuisine, with Ravjul bil-Gbejniet being a local favorite. These homemade ravioli are filled with fresh Gozitan cheeselets and served in a rich tomato sauce with a sprinkle of grated Parmesan or pecorino. It's a dish that perfectly blends Italian influence with local ingredients, making it a staple in many homes and restaurants.

For those with a sweet tooth, Imqaret is a must-try dessert. These deep-fried pastry parcels are filled with a spiced date mixture and served hot, often with a scoop of ice cream. The crispy outer layer combined with the sweet, soft filling makes for an irresistible treat.

Another local favorite is Helwa tat-Tork, a dense, sweet confection made from crushed sesame seeds, sugar, and almonds. It has a rich, nutty flavor and is often served in small slices alongside coffee or tea. It's one of those simple yet addictive desserts that you'll want to bring home as a souvenir.

Gozo's take on Kwareżimal, a traditional almond-based biscuit, is also worth trying. Originally made during Lent, these spiced, chewy biscuits are now available year-round. They are naturally sweetened with honey and orange zest, making them a slightly healthier option among Maltese sweets.

To wash it all down, Gozitan wine is a must-try. The island's small but dedicated wineries produce excellent reds, whites, and rosés, often using indigenous grape varieties. For something stronger, Bajtra Liqueur, made from prickly pears, is a uniquely Maltese drink with a sweet, slightly tangy taste.

Wine Regions and Local Breweries

Gozo may be small, but it has a thriving wine and craft beer scene that showcases the island's rich agricultural traditions. With its limestone-rich soil, mild climate, and coastal breezes, the island provides an ideal environment for grape growing, producing some exceptional wines, many of which are made in small, family-run vineyards that have been cultivating grapes for generations. In recent years, local breweries have also become increasingly popular, offering craft beers made with Gozitan ingredients.

One of the most well-known wineries on Gozo is Ta' Mena Estate, located near Xagħra. This family-run estate focuses on producing high-quality wine, olive oil, and other traditional Gozitan products. Their vineyards yield both international and indigenous grape varieties, with excellent reds, whites, and rosés. Visitors can enjoy guided tours of the vineyard, learning about the winemaking process and sampling the wines, often paired with local cheeses and cured meats. Their flagship wines include a bold Merlot and a crisp, mineral-driven Girgentina, a native white grape of Malta. Another standout producer is Tal-Massar Winery in Għarb. This winery is known for its commitment to sustainable and organic farming, producing limited batches of wines that showcase the island's agricultural potential. Their Syrah and Chardonnay blends are particularly well-regarded. The winery offers intimate tastings, where visitors can sip wine while overlooking Gozo's scenic countryside. Ta' Betta Wines is another boutique winery that blends local and international grape varieties, producing reds with deep, complex flavors and vibrant whites and rosés that reflect the island's warm climate.

The wine production in Gozo may be small-scale, but it is marked by craftsmanship and attention to detail, with many bottles remaining exclusive to the island and unavailable for export. For visitors, this makes it a special treat and an opportunity to taste unique wines that aren't easily found elsewhere.

While wine has long been part of Gozo's culture, craft beer has emerged more recently. Lord Chambray Brewery, based in Xewkija, has quickly become one of Malta and Gozo's leading craft beer producers. The brewery specializes in small-batch, handcrafted beers made with natural ingredients and traditional brewing methods. Their selection includets a variety of styles that reflect the island's Mediterranean character. The Blue Lagoon Blonde Ale is a light, refreshing beer inspired by the island's clear waters, while the San Blas English IPA offers a more hop-forward taste with a balance of bitterness and citrusy aromas. For those who enjoy richer flavors, the Fungus Rock Stout provides a maltier, deeper brew named after the iconic rock formation near Dwejra Bay. Visitors to Lord Chambray can tour the brewery, learn about the brewing process, and sample the full range of beers, making it a great way to experience the island's growing craft beer scene.

If you want to sample Gozo's wines and craft beers without visiting the vineyards or brewery directly, several bars and restaurants across the island offer excellent selections. Il-Kartell in Marsalforn features a curated list of Gozitan wines, perfect for pairing with fresh seafood or traditional Maltese dishes. In Victoria, Vinoteca is a small wine bar offering a selection of local wines by the glass, while The Boathouse in Xlendi combines Lord Chambray's craft beers with Gozitan wines, making it a perfect spot to unwind by the water. For those looking to take a piece of Gozo home, both Ta' Mena Estate and Lord Chambray Brewery offer bottled wines and beers for sale, so you can bring the island's flavors back with you.

Farmers' Markets and Food Tours

Gozo, with its fertile land and rich agricultural traditions, is a paradise for food lovers. The island's farmers' markets and food tours offer a chance to taste the freshest local produce, explore traditional flavors, and learn about the island's agricultural practices.

One of the best ways to experience Gozo's food culture is by visiting the Victoria Farmers' Market, held every Saturday morning in the heart of the island's capital. Here, locals and visitors alike gather to buy fresh fruit, vegetables, and herbs, much of which is grown on Gozo itself. The market is not only about produce; it also offers locally made cheeses, olives, honey, and cured meats, giving visitors a full spectrum of Gozitan flavors to sample. The vibrant atmosphere and the opportunity to interact with local farmers make this market an essential stop for anyone wanting to experience the island's authentic food culture.

Another great farmers' market is the Xagħra Farmers' Market, held on Sundays. This smaller market is perfect for those looking for a quieter experience while still enjoying a wide selection of fresh, locally sourced ingredients. Visitors can find organic fruits, vegetables, and fresh fish caught off the coast of Gozo, as well as hand-made pastries and traditional

Gozitan bread. It's also an ideal place to pick up artisanal products like olive oil and homemade jams that are a true reflection of Gozo's culinary heritage.

For those who want to go beyond the markets and immerse themselves in the island's food culture, a food tour of Gozo offers a deeper look at its gastronomy. Many local tour operators offer guided tours that take you through the island's picturesque villages, stopping at family-run farms, vineyards, and eateries along the way. These tours often include tastings of Gozitan specialties like Fenek Moqli (rabbit stew), Gbejniet (local cheese), and Imqaret (date pastries). During these tours, guides often share the history behind each dish and the methods used to prepare them, providing a richer understanding of Gozo's food culture.

One of the most popular food tours is the Gozo Food Tour, which takes visitors on a journey through the island's markets and traditional food establishments. The tour typically includes stops at local bakeries where you can sample fresh ftira (a traditional Maltese flatbread), cheese shops, and even vineyards where Gozitan wines are produced. The tour is a wonderful way to discover the island's authentic flavors while learning about its agricultural roots.

Another option is the Gozo Wine and Dine Tour, which focuses specifically on the island's wine and food pairings. This tour visits some of Gozo's best wineries, where you can taste locally produced wines and enjoy a meal paired with Gozitan delicacies. It's a great way to learn about the island's winemaking traditions while savoring the flavors of fresh, seasonal produce.

For a more hands-on experience, some tours also offer cooking classes, where visitors can try their hand at making Gozitan dishes themselves. These cooking classes often take place in local homes or traditional kitchens, providing an intimate and personal experience. You'll be able to learn how to prepare local favorites like Ravjul (Gozitan ravioli), Bragioli (beef olives), and Timpana (baked pasta with meat sauce).

Cooking Classes and Workshops

Gozo's culinary culture is steeped in tradition, and there's no better way to experience it than by participating in a local cooking class or workshop. Whether you're keen on mastering Gozitan dishes or learning about Mediterranean flavors, these hands-on experiences offer a genuine insight into the island's rich food heritage.

Ta' Mena Estate, located just outside Xagħra, offers some of the most popular cooking classes on the island. Known for its focus on local and organic ingredients, the estate provides an intimate, interactive experience where guests can learn how to prepare traditional Gozitan dishes such as Fenek Moqli (rabbit stew), Ravjul (Gozitan ravioli), and Timpana (baked pasta with meat sauce). The classes are held in the estate's kitchen, and participants are guided step-by-step through the preparation of each dish, before sitting down to enjoy the meal they've created. The estate also offers a tour of their vineyard, providing context on how the ingredients are sourced. These cooking sessions offer a wonderful opportunity to connect with the local food culture while enjoying the peaceful surroundings of Gozo's countryside.

For a more immersive experience, Gozo's Traditional Cooking School in Victoria offers small, personalized workshops where participants can explore the island's culinary traditions. The classes focus on preparing classic Gozitan dishes, with a particular emphasis on the use of fresh, seasonal ingredients. During these workshops, you can learn how to make everything from Gbejniet (local cheeselets) to Imqaret (date-filled pastries), all while gaining insights into the island's agricultural practices and local food production. These hands-on experiences allow you to engage with Gozo's culinary heritage, and you'll leave not only with a full belly but also with new cooking skills to take home.

The Mediterranean Cooking Experience at Gozo's Culinary Centre is another fantastic option for those wanting to expand their culinary repertoire. This class teaches traditional Mediterranean cooking techniques, with an emphasis on fresh produce, local herbs, and simple, flavorful dishes. Under the guidance of expert chefs, you'll learn to prepare a range of dishes that showcase the best of Gozo's seasonal offerings, including fish, olive oil, and fresh vegetables. The classes are often followed by a communal meal, providing an opportunity to enjoy the fruits of your labor with fellow participants.

For something a little different, Gozo Organic Farm offers a unique cooking experience that takes you directly to the source of your ingredients. The farm grows organic produce, and the cooking class includes a tour of the farm to pick fresh vegetables and herbs, which will then be used in the dishes you prepare. The focus here is on organic, sustainable cooking, and participants learn how to create dishes using fresh, local ingredients. This is a great opportunity to understand how Gozo's fertile soil and mild climate contribute to its rich culinary tradition.

Dining Etiquette Tips

Dining in Gozo is a wonderful experience, with the island's food culture grounded in tradition and hospitality. While meals are generally relaxed and unhurried, there are a few etiquette tips that can help you feel more comfortable when enjoying Gozitan cuisine.

Punctuality is important in formal dining settings, so if you're attending a dinner at a restaurant or someone's home, it's best to arrive on time. If you happen to be late, it's usually forgiven as long as you don't keep others waiting for too long. In more casual settings, such as outdoor cafés or village eateries, there is less emphasis on being exactly on time. For dress, the atmosphere in Gozo is typically casual, especially in local village cafés where t-shirts, shorts, and casual shoes are completely acceptable. However, for more upscale restaurants, particularly in Victoria or other more formal venues, smart casual attire is recommended. For special occasions like weddings or family gatherings, dressing a little more formally is a sign of respect.

When dining at the table, it's customary to keep your hands above the table, and avoid resting your elbows on the edge. The general rule of dining etiquette in Gozo follows continental style, meaning the fork is held in the left hand and the knife in the right. The utensils should be used from the outside in, with the larger ones used first, followed by the smaller ones as the meal progresses. It's also polite not to cut all your food at once but to cut a few pieces at a time as you eat. Meals in Gozo are often served family-style, with dishes placed in the center of the table for everyone to share. It's considered courteous to pass dishes around and try a little of everything. When serving yourself, take small portions to ensure there's enough for everyone else at the table. In local homes, the host typically serves the food first, and it's polite to wait for everyone to be served before beginning your meal.

Transportation & Stays

Ferries and Inter-Island Travel

Getting around Gozo and its neighboring islands is simple and efficient, with ferry services providing an easy way to travel between Malta, Gozo, and Comino. Whether you're arriving by sea or hopping between the islands for a day trip, ferry travel is the most common and scenic way to explore the region.

The Gozo Channel Ferry is the primary service connecting Gozo with mainland Malta. The ferry departs regularly from Cirkewwa on the northern tip of Malta and arrives at Mgarr in Gozo, a picturesque harbor that offers visitors their first glimpse of the island. The ferry ride takes about 25 minutes and offers stunning views of the Mediterranean Sea, with the chance to see both Malta and Gozo from the water. The ferries run every 45 minutes, with additional services during peak times, making it easy to hop between the two islands. Tickets are reasonably priced, with rates for cars, passengers, and motorbikes, allowing for flexible travel options. No reservation is required for passengers, but booking in advance is recommended if you plan to bring a vehicle during busy seasons.

For those interested in exploring Comino, the smallest of the three inhabited islands, the ferry service from Gozo to Comino is frequent and affordable. Ferries depart from Mgarr in Gozo to Santa Marija Bay or Blue Lagoon, two of the most popular spots on Comino. The short crossing only takes about 10 to 15 minutes, and tickets are typically sold on the dock. The ferries between Gozo and Comino are seasonal, running from spring to autumn, and can be especially crowded during the summer months when tourists flock to Comino's crystal-clear waters.

In addition to the regular ferry services, several private boat operators offer personalized trips around Gozo, Comino, and Malta. These private boat rides can take you to secluded beaches, caves, and lagoons that are not easily accessible by public ferry. For those looking for a more intimate experience, many of these boat tours also include stops at iconic spots such as the Blue Lagoon, Crystal Lagoon, and Caves of Comino, where you can enjoy snorkeling or simply bask in the Mediterranean sun.

Public Transport: Buses and Taxis

Public transportation in Gozo is straightforward, with both buses and taxis providing easy ways to get around the island. Though Gozo is smaller than Malta, the public transport system is reliable, and there are plenty of options for those looking to explore without needing a car.

The bus network, run by Malta Public Transport, covers the major towns and tourist attractions. The central bus terminal is located in Victoria, Gozo's capital, which acts as the main hub for departures to other destinations like Xlendi, Marsalforn, Mgarr, and the Blue Lagoon on Comino. Other routes also cover more rural areas and scenic spots like Dwejra and Ramla Bay. Buses are generally well-maintained, and the service is dependable, though the island's hilly terrain and narrow roads mean travel can be slower than on Malta. Buses run from early morning until around 6:00 PM, but they become less frequent as the day progresses, so it's advisable to plan your trips during daylight hours. Tickets are affordable, and you can buy them directly from the driver. For those staying a little longer on the island, the Gozo 7-Day Pass offers unlimited travel on the island's buses, which can be a great value.

For a more personalized and direct form of transport, taxis are a convenient choice. They're readily available in Victoria and at popular tourist spots like Xlendi Bay and Marsalforn. Many hotels and guesthouses can also arrange taxi services. Taxi fares are generally fixed, so you'll know the cost in advance, making it easier to plan your budget. Taxis are ideal for reaching remote destinations where public buses may not go, or for traveling between towns in a fraction of the time it would take by bus. Many taxi drivers also offer private tours of Gozo, where they take you around the island's highlights and hidden gems. This option is great for those looking to discover more about Gozo's culture and history while traveling in comfort.

In addition to taxis, there are other transport options, such as private car hires and shared transport services. Private vehicles can be rented for short or full-day trips, giving you the freedom to explore at your own pace. Shared transport services, like shuttle buses or ridesharing options, are also available for groups or those on a tighter budget, and are popular for trips to Comino. For more independent exploration, some visitors prefer renting bicycles or scooters, which are widely available in Victoria and Xlendi. This allows for a more flexible travel experience, especially for those who enjoy outdoor activities and want to stop along the way to take in the views or visit off-the-beaten-path spots.

Car Rentals and Road Trips

Renting a car in Gozo is a convenient way to explore the island at your own pace, allowing you to reach remote corners, scenic viewpoints, and hidden gems that might be harder to access by public transport. With its relatively small size and well-maintained roads, Gozo is perfect for a leisurely road trip, and car rentals are widely available across the island.

Most car rental agencies are located in Victoria, the capital, or at Mgarr Harbour, where ferries from Malta arrive. You'll find a variety of vehicles available, from compact cars ideal for navigating Gozo's narrow streets to larger SUVs if you plan on exploring the island's rugged terrain. Rental companies typically offer both short-term and long-term rentals, with flexible pick-up and drop-off times, making it easy to fit your travel schedule.

Driving in Gozo is generally easy, as the island is quieter and less congested compared to Malta. The roads are well-marked, but be prepared for winding, narrow lanes, especially when venturing into more rural areas. If you plan to drive to some of Gozo's remote locations, such as Ta' Cenc Cliffs, Ramla Bay, or Dwejra Bay, you'll enjoy the scenic drive through

104

countryside roads that lead to some of the island's most beautiful and unspoiled spots.

One of the highlights of renting a car is the freedom it offers to take a road trip around the island. A recommended route starts with a visit to the Cittadella in Victoria, where you can enjoy panoramic views of Gozo. From there, you can drive to Xlendi, a charming coastal village with a picturesque bay that's perfect for a relaxing stop. Afterward, head north to Marsalforn, another coastal gem, where you can enjoy seafood by the water. Make sure to check out Ramla Bay on your way, with its unique red sand and clear waters.

For a more adventurous drive, head towards Dwejra Bay, where you can see the remains of the Azure Window and explore the Inland Sea. The roads here are more rugged, and you'll pass through some of Gozo's most dramatic landscapes, so it's a great option for those who love a bit of exploration. Don't forget to stop at Wied il-Mielah, where you can take in the impressive natural rock arch and enjoy the tranquility of the area.

If you're looking to make the most of your car rental, consider driving to Għarb to visit the Ta' Pinu Sanctuary, a spiritual site with stunning views of the island. Or take a detour to Xagħra, where you can visit the Ġgantija Temples, one of

Malta's most significant archaeological sites. These sites are a little further out, and having a car gives you the flexibility to visit them without worrying about public transport schedules.

As for parking, it's generally easy to find spots in the main towns, though it can be a bit busier in Victoria and near the more popular tourist destinations, especially during the summer months. Some areas, like Xlendi and Marsalforn, may have limited parking near the beach, so it's a good idea to arrive early during peak times. When parking on the streets, always check for any parking restrictions to avoid fines.

For those staying longer in Gozo, renting a car is not only useful for getting around but also for enjoying spontaneous trips to the many beautiful beaches, including secluded coves and remote countryside areas that may not be easily reached by bus. With a car, you can take in Gozo's natural beauty, from its dramatic cliffs to its serene bays, all at your own pace.

Accommodation Options

When it comes to accommodation in Gozo, there's a wide range of options that cater to every type of traveler, whether you're after a cozy guesthouse, a charming boutique hotel, or a luxurious resort. Many of Gozo's accommodations reflect the island's blend of rustic charm and modern comforts, offering a warm, welcoming atmosphere with stunning views of the countryside or coastline.

In Victoria, the island's capital, you'll find a variety of options, from intimate B&Bs to larger hotels. The Duke Boutique Hotel, located on Republic Street, offers a stylish stay right in the heart of the city. This contemporary hotel is known for its clean, modern design, offering rooms with views of the town or the surrounding hills. Prices here range from €70-€150 per night, depending on the season, with breakfast included. It's an ideal choice for those who want to be close to local restaurants, shops, and cultural attractions like the Cittadella. The hotel's restaurant also offers Mediterranean cuisine, perfect for a relaxing evening after a day of exploring. The hotel is open year-round, with check-in typically available from 2:00 PM.

For a more tranquil escape, Ta' Ċenċ Hotel & Spa offers a luxurious retreat just outside Xagħra. Set on a cliffside with panoramic views of the island's rugged coast, this five-star resort offers a range of accommodation options, including spacious rooms, suites, and private villas. Prices here start at around €150 per night, with additional fees for spa treatments or meals at the on-site restaurant. The property is perfect for those looking for relaxation, with a full-service spa, outdoor pool, and fitness center. While it's more upscale, it provides a peaceful atmosphere away from the bustle of the main towns. Open year-round, the hotel offers a tranquil getaway with all the amenities one might need for a relaxing stay. Check-in typically begins at 3:00 PM.

For those looking for a more local and homey experience, Dar ta' Ninette in Għarb is an excellent option. This charming guesthouse is housed in a traditional Gozitan building, offering a more personal and intimate experience. It's just a short drive from the iconic Ta' Pinu Sanctuary and offers cozy rooms decorated in a rustic style, with modern touches. Prices for a night here start from €60-€100, depending on the season. The guesthouse is known for its hospitality, and the owner often provides local tips on what to see and do around the island. Breakfast is served daily, and guests can enjoy a quiet garden space. Dar ta' Ninette is open throughout the year, with check-in available from 12:00 PM.

If you prefer a more modern and convenient option, Hotel Calypso in Marsalforn offers a comfortable stay near the island's popular beach. This hotel provides easy access to the beach, restaurants, and shops of the area. The rooms here have simple, clean decor with balconies that overlook the Mediterranean Sea. Nightly rates range from €80 to €120, depending on the season. This is an excellent choice for those looking to combine relaxation by the beach with proximity to local dining and activities. The hotel is open year-round, with check-in available from 2:00 PM.

For travelers who enjoy a more hands-on experience, Gozo Farmhouses offers a unique accommodation option. These traditional properties, scattered across Gozo, allow guests to experience island life in a more intimate setting. Most farmhouses feature private pools, spacious courtyards, and easy access to the countryside. Prices vary based on the location and size of the farmhouse but typically range from €100 to €250 per night for a family-sized house. These properties are perfect for larger groups or families, offering a fully equipped kitchen, making it easy to prepare meals using fresh, local ingredients. Many of the farmhouses are available for rent year-round, with flexible check-in times.

Unique Lodging Experiences

Gozo offers a variety of unique lodging experiences that allow visitors to immerse themselves in the island's charm and history while enjoying comfort and character. Whether you're looking for a stay in a historic building, a rural retreat, or a stay by the sea, Gozo has accommodations that provide a distinctive sense of place.

One of the most special ways to experience Gozo is by staying in a traditional farmhouse. These charming properties are scattered throughout the island, often surrounded by fields and olive groves. Many of the farmhouses date back centuries, offering a combination of rustic stone walls and modern amenities. Some, like those in Għarb and Xagħra, feature private pools and outdoor spaces with stunning views of the countryside. Prices for farmhouses vary, typically starting from €100 per night for a smaller property, with larger houses going up to €250 or more. The sense of living like a local, with space to cook your meals and enjoy Gozo's tranquil rural surroundings, is a truly unique experience. Most farmhouses are available for year-round rentals, with flexible check-in and check-out times.

For those looking for a more intimate experience, boutique hotels in Gozo offer a perfect mix of style, comfort, and local flair. The House of Phyllis in Victoria is a small, family-run hotel with just a handful of rooms, each one uniquely decorated with a blend of modern and vintage furniture. The house is set in a charming alley, offering an escape from the busy town, yet it's just a short walk from the Cittadella and local restaurants. Prices typically range from €80-€150 per night, depending on the room and season. Staying here feels like visiting a friend's house, where personalized service and attention to detail make the stay memorable.

For something truly offbeat, the Ta' Cenc Eco Village offers an eco-friendly retreat that allows you to experience Gozo's natural beauty while being mindful of the environment. The eco-village consists of small, traditional Gozitan cottages nestled into the hillside near Xagħra, offering a peaceful retreat with panoramic views of the surrounding countryside. The cottages are self-sustained with solar panels, water-saving features, and a commitment to sustainability, making it a great option for eco-conscious travelers. Prices here start at around €90 per night, with the added benefit of learning about local sustainable farming practices and eco-living. The village is perfect for those looking to disconnect and embrace a slower pace of life.

For a more luxurious, unique experience, The Phoenicia Malta, located in the heart of the capital, offers a blend of classic elegance and modern comfort. While technically in Malta, it's easily accessible from Gozo, and offers a higher-end experience that features stunning views of the Grand Harbour, an exquisite spa, and fine dining options. It's ideal for those wanting to explore both islands, while staying in a glamorous, historic hotel. Rooms start at €250 per night, offering a chic escape with easy access to both cultural landmarks and the island's natural beauty.

Finally, cliffside accommodations like those at The View Hotel in Xlendi Bay offer some of the best views on Gozo. With rooms overlooking the crystal-clear waters of Xlendi Bay, this hotel provides a stunning setting for both relaxation and exploration. Guests can enjoy easy access to the beach, plus a variety of waterfront dining options. This is ideal for those looking to combine natural beauty with modern comfort, as well as those eager to explore the surrounding beaches and hiking trails. Room rates here typically start from €100 per night.

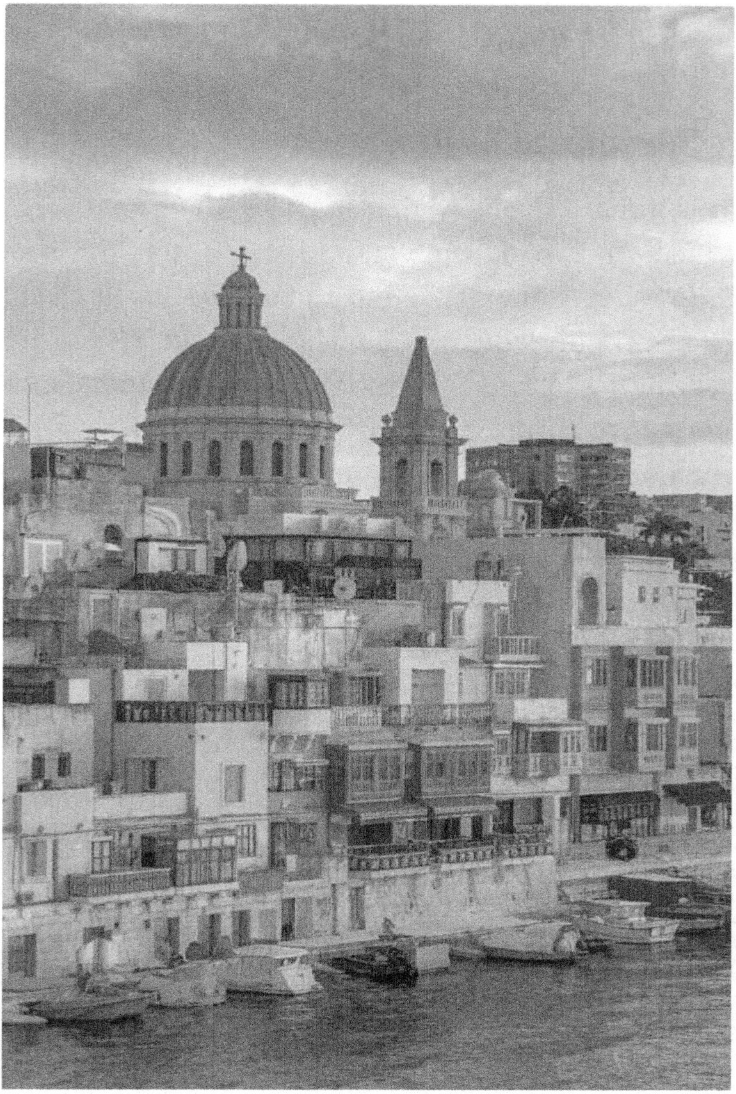

Travel Tips & Safety

Best Seasons to Visit

The best time to visit Malta and Gozo largely depends on what kind of experience you're looking for. Spring, from March to May, is one of the most ideal seasons to visit, as the weather is comfortably warm, ranging from 15°C (59°F) in early spring to 25°C (77°F) by May. The countryside blooms with wildflowers, providing a beautiful backdrop for hiking and outdoor activities. During this time, Malta's cultural scene comes alive with local celebrations and festivals, such as the Good Friday processions. The crowds are manageable, allowing for a more relaxed exploration of the islands and their key attractions.

Summer, spanning from June to August, brings the warmest temperatures, ranging from 30°C (86°F) to 35°C (95°F). This is the peak tourist season, with Malta and Gozo buzzing with activity, especially around the beaches. The waters are perfect for swimming, diving, and snorkeling, and it's the time when many outdoor events and festivals, such as the Malta International Arts Festival, take place. However, it can get crowded, particularly in popular tourist spots, and prices are at their highest. If you don't mind the heat and the crowds, summer offers a lively atmosphere, great for those looking for sun and beach days.

Autumn, from September to November, is often considered the best time to visit. The weather remains warm, with temperatures between 20°C (68°F) and 30°C (86°F), but without the intensity of the summer heat. The island is quieter, as the crowds from peak season start to thin out, making it ideal for a more peaceful visit. The sea stays warm enough for swimming, and the islands' natural landscapes remain lush from the summer rains. September also hosts some important local events like the Feast of Our Lady of Victories in Victoria, offering a chance to experience Malta's traditions. For food and wine lovers, autumn is harvest time, and you can explore vineyards and farms busy with grape picking and olive harvesting.

Winter, from December to February, is the quietest season, with temperatures ranging from 10°C (50°F) to 15°C (59°F). While it may be too cold for beach days, the weather is still comfortable enough for sightseeing and outdoor activities. During this period, the islands feel much quieter, and you can enjoy the historical sites and natural beauty without the crowds. Some outdoor attractions may close during the off-season, but cultural sites and museums remain open, offering a more relaxed experience. The holiday season, especially Christmas, brings a special charm to the islands, with fewer tourists but a warm, festive atmosphere. While Malta and Gozo are not tropical destinations during the winter, the islands still offer plenty for visitors seeking peace and solitude.

Budgeting and Saving Money

When visiting Gozo and Malta, it's possible to enjoy all the beauty, history, and culture of the islands without breaking the bank. The key is knowing where to spend and where to save, and with a little planning, you can make the most of your trip while keeping costs down.

Accommodation in Gozo offers a variety of choices for budget-conscious travelers. Opting for guesthouses or bed and breakfasts in smaller towns like Xagħra or Għarb can save you money, and you'll still be close to the island's main attractions. Prices typically range from €50 to €90 per night, depending on the season. Booking ahead, especially during the shoulder seasons like late spring or early autumn, can help you secure lower rates. If you're staying in Victoria, where prices can be higher, consider booking a little outside the city center for more affordable options.

When it comes to eating, local eateries and small cafes offer affordable meals that still provide an authentic taste of Gozo's food culture. For example, Xlendi Bay and Marsalforn have plenty of casual spots where you can grab a bite without spending a fortune. Street food like pastizzi (flaky pastries filled with ricotta or peas) is not only a delicious snack but also very cheap, often costing just a couple of euros. Enjoying fresh fish at the seaside is also possible on a budget, particularly in smaller, family-run restaurants where you'll get the best value for your money. Dining out in more touristy areas or upscale restaurants will, of course, cost more, so it's good to know where the locals eat if you want to keep costs in check.

For getting around the island, public transportation in Gozo is budget-friendly. Buses are the main mode of travel, with tickets costing around €1.50 for a single ride. If you plan to explore multiple areas, consider purchasing a 7-day bus pass for about €10, which gives you unlimited access to the island's bus network. The buses can be a bit slower due to the winding roads, but they offer a great way to see the island and are much cheaper than taxis or car rentals. If you prefer to have more flexibility or plan to visit some of the more remote areas, renting a car is an option, but it can be pricier. It's often cheaper to rent a car for a couple of days rather than the entire trip, especially if you plan on using public transport for the rest of your stay.

One of the best ways to save money while sightseeing is to buy passes or tickets in advance for multiple attractions. For instance, if you're planning to visit the Ġgantija Temples and other museums, check if there's a combined ticket offering discounts. Many attractions also offer student or senior discounts, so if that applies to you, make sure to ask.

Another good way to keep your budget in check is to take advantage of the natural beauty of Gozo and Malta. Both islands offer stunning scenery, from Ramla Bay and Dwejra Bay to the Cittadella in Victoria, and many of these sights are free to enjoy. Hiking is also a great way to explore Gozo, with various trails offering incredible views at no cost. Whether you're walking along the coastline or hiking through the countryside, the natural landscape is one of the best experiences you can have without spending any money.

For those interested in day trips, consider taking the Gozo ferry from Malta, which is a cost-effective way to visit the island. The ferry ride is just 25 minutes long and costs around €4 for a round trip, and while it's a popular route, it's not expensive compared to other transport options.

Health and Safety Advice

When visiting Gozo and Malta, staying safe and healthy is essential to making the most of your trip. While the islands are generally safe, like any travel destination, there are a few things to keep in mind to ensure a smooth and enjoyable experience.

First and foremost, sun protection is a must. Malta and Gozo are known for their sunny weather, especially during the summer months, so it's easy to get burned if you're not careful. Be sure to wear sunscreen with a high SPF, and apply it regularly throughout the day, even if you're not swimming or lying directly in the sun. Wearing a hat and sunglasses is also a good idea, especially if you plan to spend a lot of time outdoors. The sun can be intense, so take breaks in the shade to avoid overheating.

If you're visiting during the warmer months, hydration is crucial. The Mediterranean climate can make the heat feel even more intense, and it's easy to get dehydrated, especially if you're walking around the islands or spending time on the beaches. Keep a bottle of water with you and drink frequently, even if you're not thirsty. Many shops and cafés sell bottled water, and you'll also find water fountains in some tourist spots.

In terms of medical care, Gozo has several pharmacies, especially in Victoria and Xlendi, where you can get over-the-counter medicines or seek advice on minor health issues. The island also has a public hospital, Gozo General Hospital, which provides emergency medical services. For more serious health concerns, there are medical centers and clinics around Malta as well, but it's wise to have travel insurance that covers medical emergencies just in case.

Insect repellent can be handy, particularly if you're spending time near nature reserves or in rural areas, as mosquitoes and other bugs can be more active in the evening. Be sure to pack some repellent if you're prone to bites or if you plan to hike in nature reserves, where the local wildlife is more abundant.

On the roads, driving is on the left side, so if you're renting a car or scooter, take extra care to adjust to the local traffic rules. The roads are generally well-maintained, but some of the rural paths can be narrow or winding, so always drive cautiously. If you're renting a scooter or bicycle, wear a helmet for safety, as some areas can be steep or challenging for less experienced riders.

For those looking to swim or dive, sea safety is always important. The waters around Gozo can be beautiful, but they can also be deceptively deep or rocky in certain areas. Always swim at designated beaches, where lifeguards are on duty, and check local weather and sea conditions before heading out. When snorkeling or diving, ensure you're with a reputable company that provides safety briefings and equipment, especially if you're not familiar with the waters.

Cultural Do's and Don'ts

When visiting Gozo and Malta, understanding the local culture and traditions will help you have a more respectful and enjoyable experience. Maltese culture is shaped by centuries of history, blending Mediterranean, European, and North African influences, and the people are known for their warmth and hospitality. However, like any place, there are some cultural norms and expectations to keep in mind.

Maltese people take great pride in their cultural heritage and traditions, so it's important to show respect for their customs. If you're invited to a local family gathering or religious celebration, it's polite to accept the invitation, as hospitality is a significant part of Maltese life. When visiting churches, cathedrals, or religious sites, it's customary to dress modestly, covering your shoulders and knees, as a sign of respect for the sacred space. This also applies to some museums and heritage sites where a more formal atmosphere may be observed.

A simple greeting in Maltese, such as "Bongu" (Good morning) or "Kif inti?" (How are you?), can go a long way in fostering goodwill. While many people in Gozo and Malta speak English, making an effort to greet them in their native language is appreciated, even if it's just a few words.

While tipping isn't mandatory, it's a common practice in Gozo and Malta. It's customary to leave a small tip in restaurants, cafes, and to taxi drivers when you receive good service. It's a sign of appreciation for the hospitality and service you've received, and locals generally expect tips for services rendered, though it's entirely up to you how much you leave.

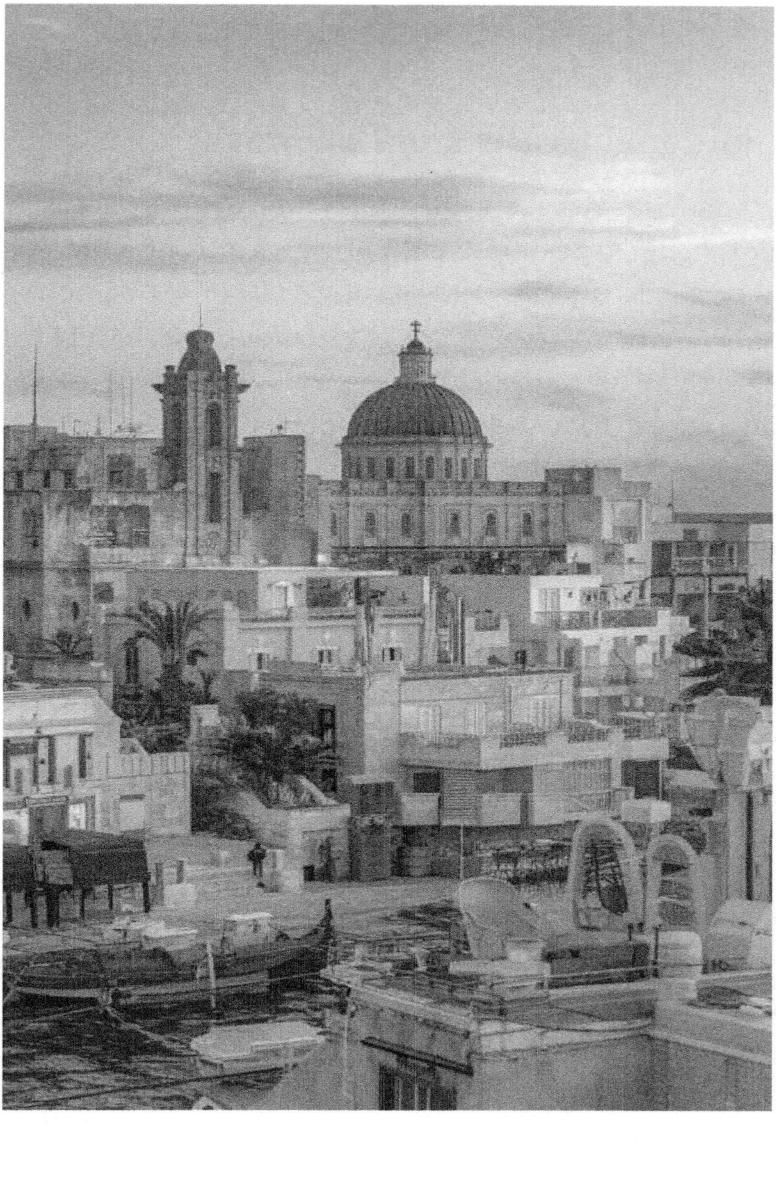

Shopping & Souvenirs

Traditional Crafts and Lacework

Gozo and Malta have a long tradition of craftsmanship, and one of the most beautiful and intricate forms of artistry found on the islands is lacework. The craft dates back centuries and is still a vibrant part of Maltese culture today. The art of Maltese lace is renowned for its delicate patterns and fine detail, which have been passed down through generations. You can find beautiful examples of lacework in shops, markets, and artisan workshops across Gozo, with local women continuing the tradition of creating these masterpieces by hand.

The most well-known type of lace from the islands is Maltese lace, which consists of intricate floral and geometric designs. Historically, the craft was introduced to the islands by the Knights of St. John, who brought lace-making techniques from Italy and other European countries. Today, lacework is produced using a technique called bobbin lace, where threads are wound around wooden bobbins to form elaborate patterns. The lace is then carefully stitched together to create delicate scarves, tablecloths, handkerchiefs, and other decorative items.

A visit to Victoria, the capital of Gozo, offers the chance to witness traditional lacework being created. Some local shops and craft studios still sell handmade lace products, and if you're interested in learning about the process, you can even visit workshops where artisans demonstrate their techniques. These handcrafted pieces are not just souvenirs, but intricate works of art that reflect the island's rich cultural heritage.

In addition to lacework, Gozo is also home to other traditional crafts, including pottery and woodworking. Local potters produce beautiful ceramics with earthy colors and simple, yet elegant, designs that reflect the island's rural traditions. These pieces are often decorated with motifs inspired by nature, such as flowers, birds, and marine life, and are sold in local galleries and artisan shops.

The island's woodworking tradition is another testament to its craftsmanship. Many skilled artisans craft furniture, home decor items, and ornamental pieces using locally sourced materials like olive wood and pine. These wooden creations are often made by hand, showcasing intricate carving techniques and attention to detail.

Best Markets and Shopping Streets

Gozo offers a charming mix of traditional markets, local artisan shops, and unique boutiques that provide visitors with a chance to explore the island's culture and take home something special. The markets are a fantastic way to experience the local way of life and find handmade goods, fresh produce, and souvenirs that reflect Gozo's rich heritage.

The Victoria Market, located in the heart of the island's capital, is one of the best places to soak in the local atmosphere. Open every morning, except Sundays, this vibrant market is a mix of fresh fruit, vegetables, and local delicacies, as well as flowers, spices, and handmade goods. Here, you can stroll through aisles of colorful stalls, where vendors sell everything from locally grown tomatoes and olives to freshly baked bread and cheeses. The market is a great place to pick up ingredients for a picnic or sample some of the island's fresh produce. It's not just for food lovers—there are also small shops selling handmade pottery, lacework, and traditional Gozitan crafts, making it a perfect spot to find a unique souvenir.

Republic Street in Victoria is another top destination for shopping. This bustling pedestrian street is lined with boutiques, souvenir shops, and artisanal stores. You'll find a variety of local products, including Maltese lace, pottery, and handcrafted jewelry. It's a great place to pick up something that showcases the island's traditions, or to simply wander and explore the lively atmosphere. The street is also home to several cafes where you can take a break and people-watch, making it an excellent area to spend some time in the heart of the island's cultural hub.

For those seeking more upscale shopping or unique designer items, Marsalforn offers a selection of boutique shops and galleries that feature local designers and craftspeople. Many of the shops here sell high-quality leather goods, clothing, and accessories, often made by local artisans. It's a quieter alternative to the busy streets of Victoria, and its seaside location adds a peaceful vibe to the shopping experience.

If you're in the mood for antiques or something with a bit more history, head to Xlendi where you'll find small, charming shops offering vintage items and antique furniture. This coastal village is known for its scenic beauty, but it also has a few stores where you can browse unique pieces that have been sourced from around the island.

Local Delicacies to Bring Home

When you visit Gozo, picking up a few local delicacies is the perfect way to take a piece of the island's rich culture and flavors home with you. With a mix of Mediterranean influences and Gozitan agricultural traditions, there's an abundance of authentic foods to choose from that make for memorable souvenirs.

Gbejniet, the island's beloved cheeselets, are one of the most iconic local delicacies. Made from sheep's milk, these small, round cheeses come in a variety of types. The fresh version is soft and mild, while the aged one has a firmer texture and a more robust flavor. You can also find peppered Gbejniet, where the cheese is coated in peppercorns for an extra kick. These cheeses are widely available in markets and shops and are perfect for snacking or adding to meals.

Another staple that you won't want to miss is Gozo honey. Known for its distinct flavor, this honey is produced by local bees that collect nectar from the island's thyme flowers. It has a subtle, herbal taste and is often sold in beautifully packaged jars, making it not only a treat for your tastebuds but also a lovely gift to bring home. It's versatile enough for use in cooking, as a topping for bread, or sweetening drinks like tea.

Gozo olive oil is also a standout product. The island has a long history of olive cultivation, and the local olive oils are a great reflection of that heritage. The oils are cold-pressed, resulting in a rich, full-bodied taste that's perfect for drizzling over salads, using in cooking, or simply dipping bread. Bottles of this high-quality olive oil often come in stylish packaging, making them both practical and aesthetically pleasing gifts.

For those with a sweet tooth, Imqaret are a must-try. These deep-fried pastries are filled with a sweet date mixture and spiced with a variety of local herbs. Although they're typically enjoyed fresh, they are often sold in packs, making them easy to bring home. Their rich, spiced filling offers a true taste of Gozo's traditional flavors.

Another popular sweet treat is Malta's nougat. Made with honey, almonds, and sugar, this chewy candy is a favorite across the Maltese islands. It often comes in different varieties, including chocolate-coated versions, and is commonly sold in colorful wrapping. Nougat is an excellent gift for anyone with a sweet tooth and is a delicious way to share a taste of Gozo's culinary traditions.

Finally, Bajtra Liqueur, a prickly pear-based drink, is a unique specialty of Gozo. This liqueur has a sweet, tangy taste and a striking pink color, making it a fun souvenir to bring back. It's typically served after meals and is a great conversation starter with friends or family.

Antique and Vintage Hunting

Gozo offers a unique treasure trove for antique and vintage lovers, with its blend of historical richness and local craftsmanship. Whether you're a seasoned collector or just curious about the island's past, you'll find charming antique shops and vintage markets tucked away in villages and towns across the island. The hunt for timeless items is part of the thrill, and exploring Gozo's antiques scene is a journey into its history and culture.

In Victoria, the island's capital, you'll find a variety of small shops offering antiques that reflect Gozo's past. Many of these stores are family-run, and you can often chat with the owners who are knowledgeable about the pieces they sell. From furniture to artwork, you'll discover items that have been lovingly preserved and restored. Antique wooden furniture, often made from local materials like olive wood, is particularly popular and gives a glimpse into Gozitan homes of the past. Many pieces are intricately carved and make for beautiful decorative items or functional heirlooms.

If you're seeking something more specific, such as vintage jewelry or collectible coins, you can often find these treasures in smaller shops near the main streets of Republic Street or Independence Square. Look out for unique items, like old Maltese coins or silverware, which make excellent souvenirs or additions to a collection.

In Xlendi, a quieter spot known for its stunning coastal views, you may come across quaint little antique shops filled with a variety of vintage goods. Here, you'll often find old maps, photographs, and traditional ceramics that reflect Gozo's rich maritime history. These shops can feel like mini-museums, filled with items that tell the story of Gozo's past. Some stores specialize in vintage ceramics, featuring designs and styles passed down through generations, often showcasing the unique craftsmanship of Gozitan artisans.

For those looking for a more diverse selection, Marsalforn also offers a mix of antique and second-hand shops. The small village is home to several places that specialize in vintage furniture, paintings, and pottery. If you're willing to dig through these quirky stores, you'll likely find pieces that can't be found anywhere else. Many of the items here come from personal collections or estates, making each find unique.

Another great place to hunt for antiques is Għarb, a village steeped in history, where you'll often find vintage treasures at local markets. These markets tend to pop up during seasonal festivals or specific days of the week, and they offer a variety of antiques and vintage finds, from old farming tools to traditional lace. Browsing these markets gives you the chance to find something truly one-of-a-kind.

Ethical Shopping Guide

Gozo offers a variety of ethical shopping options for those who want to support local artisans, promote sustainable practices, and purchase products that have a positive impact on the environment and the community. The island's rich cultural heritage, combined with its growing focus on sustainability, means that ethical shopping is not only possible but also an integral part of the local economy. One of the best ways to shop ethically on Gozo is by purchasing locally-made items that reflect the island's unique traditions. Handmade lacework, pottery, and wooden crafts are just a few examples of products that carry the signature of Gozitan artisans. These goods are often crafted by small family-run businesses or individual artisans who take pride in preserving their cultural heritage. Not only do you get to take home something truly special, but you're also supporting the livelihoods of local creators.

For a great selection of locally-made goods, head to Victoria, where you'll find boutique stores and markets offering handcrafted lace and pottery. Each piece tells a story of Gozo's past, and many of these products are made using traditional methods that have been passed down for generations. By buying these items, you're investing in the preservation of these skills and ensuring that they continue to thrive for future generations.

The fashion industry has a significant environmental footprint, but Gozo offers some sustainable options for those looking to reduce their impact. Many local boutiques focus on offering eco-friendly, ethically sourced clothing. These shops often carry garments made from organic fabrics, locally sourced materials, or recycled fibers. Ethical fashion is becoming increasingly popular on the island, and the stores often prioritize quality over quantity, which means you can find unique, well-made items that won't end up contributing to the fast fashion cycle.

Marsalforn and Xlendi are good places to look for sustainable fashion boutiques. Many of the clothing stores here focus on handmade or vintage clothing, offering one-of-a-kind pieces that are less likely to be mass-produced. By choosing to shop at these stores, you are not only supporting eco-conscious brands but also contributing to a fashion industry that prioritizes environmental responsibility and fair working conditions.

For those interested in healthier, environmentally-friendly products, Gozo has a range of shops that offer organic and eco-conscious options. Local organic farms often sell their produce directly to consumers in markets or small shops around the island. Products such as fresh fruits and vegetables, olive oil, and herbal teas can be found in these stores, many of which are sustainably farmed and free from pesticides or chemicals. Gozo's honey is another popular organic product, known for its distinct, floral flavor. You can find these local, eco-friendly products in farmers' markets or specialty stores, contributing to the sustainability of the island's farming practices.

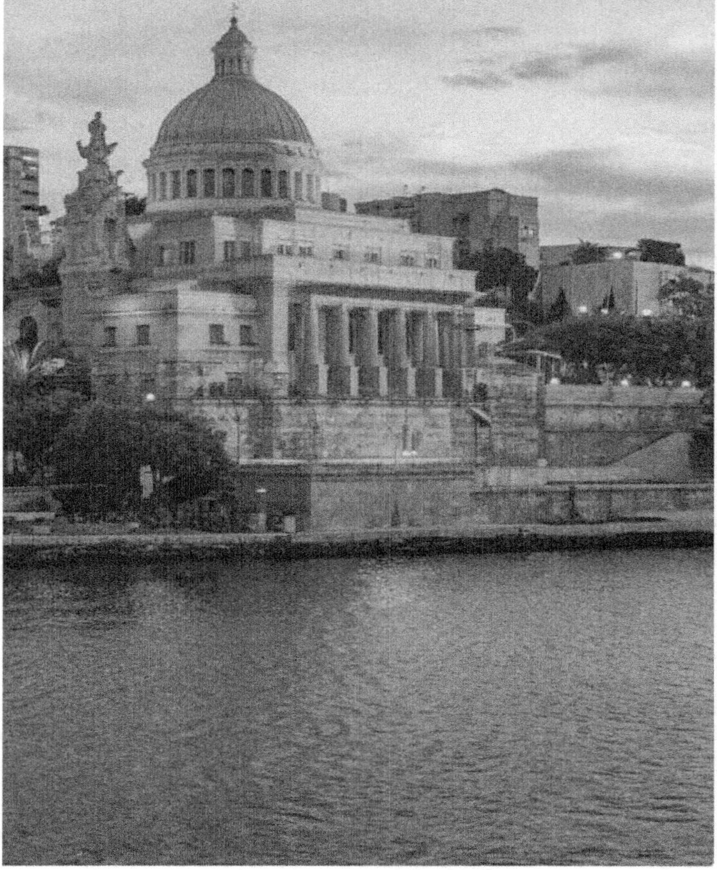

Nightlife and Hidden Gems

Popular Nightclubs and Bars

Gozo, while known for its laid-back atmosphere and scenic beauty, also offers a lively nightlife scene, particularly in the summer months. Though it's not as bustling as Malta in terms of large-scale nightlife, the island has a handful of charming bars and clubs where you can enjoy a drink, dance, or simply relax with the locals.

In Victoria, the island's capital, you'll find a number of cozy bars and pubs that serve as gathering spots for both locals and visitors. The Pub, located on Republic Street, is a popular choice for those looking for a casual night out. The atmosphere here is friendly and relaxed, and it's a great place to mingle with locals while enjoying a wide selection of drinks. The pub also frequently hosts live music, creating a fun, vibrant vibe. For a more upscale option, The Grapes Wine Bar offers a selection of local and international wines in a cozy, intimate setting. It's perfect for a quiet drink or a relaxed evening with friends.

If you're looking for a more energetic night out, Xlendi has a few options that cater to those wanting to dance or enjoy a cocktail by the sea. Café del Mar in Xlendi is one of the most well-known spots, especially during the summer, where DJs spin upbeat tracks in a trendy, beachside atmosphere. The bar offers a mix of classic cocktails and creative drinks, making it a great place to start your night before heading out to more active venues. The outdoor seating gives you a chance to enjoy your drink with a view of the bay.

For those who enjoy a lively club atmosphere, La Grotta in Xlendi is one of the island's most famous nightclubs, drawing a crowd during the warmer months. This cavernous venue offers a mixture of live DJ sets, themed nights, and parties that appeal to a younger crowd. With its outdoor terrace overlooking the sea, it's a great spot for those who want to dance the night away or just enjoy the music in a lively, open-air setting.

In Marsalforn, the nightlife is more laid-back but still offers a few bars and lounges where you can enjoy a drink or listen to live music. The Salt Bar is one of the favorite spots for both locals and tourists, offering a casual atmosphere with good music, cocktails, and a stunning view of the bay.

Live Music and Entertainment

Gozo, with its relaxed atmosphere and scenic beauty, still has a surprisingly vibrant live music and entertainment scene, especially during the warmer months. While the island doesn't boast the high-energy clubs found in larger cities, there are plenty of places where you can enjoy live performances, ranging from local bands and solo musicians to more casual acoustic sessions.

In Victoria, the island's capital, there are several venues that host live music, especially in the evenings. The Pub on Republic Street is one of the best spots for enjoying live performances. Known for its cozy, welcoming atmosphere, The Pub often features local bands and solo artists playing a mix of genres, from folk and rock to acoustic covers. The casual vibe and friendly crowd make it a great place to unwind after a day of exploring the island. You can often find music here in the evenings, particularly on weekends.

For those who enjoy a more intimate live music experience, The Grapes Wine Bar offers a selection of local wines along with live acoustic sets in a cozy, relaxed environment. It's a perfect spot to enjoy a quiet evening of music while sipping on a glass of wine, especially if you're looking for something a little more laid-back.

In Xlendi, the coastal village that's known for its charm, Café del Mar is a popular spot for live music during the summer months. Located by the sea, it attracts both locals and tourists who come to enjoy the combination of good music, cocktails, and stunning views. You'll find everything from acoustic sets to DJ performances, creating a lively but laid-back atmosphere perfect for spending the evening by the water.

If you're looking for something with a bit more energy, La Grotta in Xlendi is the place to be. Known for its cavernous space and outdoor terrace overlooking the sea, La Grotta is one of the island's top nightclubs and regularly features live DJ sets, themed nights, and parties. While it's primarily a nightclub, it also hosts live music performances that range from popular covers to electronic beats. This venue tends to attract a younger crowd, and the lively music and outdoor setting make it a memorable spot for a night out.

Throughout the summer, Gozo also hosts several festivals and events that feature live music performances, ranging from classical to contemporary styles. The Gozo Music Festival, held annually in the capital, is a highlight for music lovers, with concerts held in various venues across the island. You'll hear everything from orchestras to local bands and solo artists, making it a great opportunity to experience the island's cultural diversity through music. Similarly, Maltese folk music and traditional performances can often be found at local festivals, adding a cultural touch to the island's lively entertainment scene.

Secluded Spots and Nature Trails

Gozo is an island that boasts plenty of hidden gems, with secluded spots and nature trails that invite visitors to explore its rugged landscapes and serene beauty. Whether you're a keen hiker, nature enthusiast, or someone looking for a peaceful escape, Gozo offers numerous tranquil areas to immerse yourself in the natural surroundings.

One of the most serene and secluded spots on the island is Wied il-Mielah. Tucked away in the northwest of Gozo, this hidden valley is home to a stunning natural rock arch, similar to the famous Azure Window, which collapsed in 2017. The area is quiet, with only a handful of visitors, and is a perfect spot for those who enjoy the peaceful atmosphere of a hidden cove. You can explore the coastal cliffs here and watch the waves crash against the rocks below. It's a great location for photography, nature walks, or simply taking in the spectacular views over the Mediterranean Sea.

Another off-the-beaten-path destination is Ramla Bay, one of Gozo's most beautiful beaches, known for its reddish sand.

While it can be a bit busier during peak season, it still retains an atmosphere of tranquility, especially if you visit early in the morning or late in the afternoon. The bay is surrounded by stunning cliffs and lush greenery, making it a perfect place to relax or take a swim. The surrounding area also offers a range of nature trails, including a path that leads to Calypso Cave, which is steeped in local legend and offers panoramic views of the bay.

For those looking to get deeper into nature, the Ta' Cenc Cliffs in the south of Gozo offer some of the island's most dramatic scenery. The cliffs rise high above the sea, offering sweeping views of the coastline and the open waters below. This area is often quieter than other popular spots on Gozo, providing an ideal setting for a peaceful walk along the cliffs, or simply to sit and enjoy the stunning views. You may even spot some rare bird species, as the cliffs are home to various seabirds. The surrounding trails take you through lush greenery and offer multiple vantage points of the cliffs and the sea beyond.

Dwejra Bay is another secluded spot that offers natural beauty, with its famous Inland Sea and the Blue Hole dive site. While Dwejra is a popular spot for divers, its natural wonders and the surrounding area remain relatively untouched. You can take a peaceful boat ride through the Inland Sea or wander along the coastline, where you'll encounter dramatic cliffs, isolated beaches, and pristine waters. The area has an otherworldly feel, making it one of Gozo's most captivating natural locations.

For a truly off-the-radar experience, the Għarb countryside offers a quieter, more rural side of Gozo. The area is dotted with traditional farmhouses, olive groves, and fields of wildflowers. Wander along the country lanes, where you'll be greeted by the smell of fresh herbs and wild plants, and you may find yourself completely alone, surrounded only by nature. The area is also home to the Ta' Pinu Sanctuary, a popular religious site, which is worth visiting for its peaceful atmosphere and panoramic views of the island.

Unique Local Experiences

Gozo is more than just an island of beaches and historical sites—it's a place where visitors can immerse themselves in unique local experiences that reflect the island's culture, traditions, and way of life. Whether it's spending time with local artisans, joining a village festa, or exploring the island's landscapes in a different way, there are plenty of ways to connect with Gozo beyond the usual tourist spots.

One of the most authentic experiences on the island is joining a traditional Gozitan festa. Every village in Gozo has its own religious celebration, usually dedicated to its patron saint, and these events are some of the most vibrant cultural gatherings on the island. Expect fireworks, brass bands, processions, and a lively atmosphere as the entire community comes together to celebrate. The festas often include food stalls selling local delicacies, making it the perfect time to try traditional sweets like Imqaret (date pastries) and Qubbajt (Maltese nougat). The most famous festas take place during the summer months, with the feast of Santa Marija in Victoria being one of the most spectacular.

For those looking to get hands-on with Gozitan traditions, spending time with local artisans is a rewarding way to experience the island's creative heritage. Gozo is known for its lace-making tradition, and visiting a lace-making workshop in Victoria or Għarb allows you to see skilled craftswomen at work. Some artisans even offer short workshops where you can try your hand at making lace or pottery, giving you a deeper appreciation of these centuries-old crafts.

Food lovers can take their experience a step further by joining a traditional Gozitan cooking class. Many local farms and family-run kitchens offer workshops where you can learn to make dishes like Ravjul (Gozitan-style ravioli stuffed with local cheese) or Fenek Moqli (rabbit stew). These cooking classes usually involve a visit to a local market or farm, where you'll pick fresh ingredients before learning how to prepare the meal. It's a fantastic way to not only enjoy great food but also understand the island's culinary traditions from the people who have perfected them.

Another unique way to experience Gozo is by exploring the island's landscapes in an unconventional way. Horseback riding along the cliffs of Sanap or Dwejra is an unforgettable experience, offering breathtaking views of the coastline while riding through unspoiled countryside. Several stables offer guided rides, making it accessible even for those with little or no riding experience. Alternatively, for those who prefer something with a bit more adrenaline, quad biking tours provide an adventurous way to see the island's more remote areas, from rugged coastal paths to hidden valleys that are off the usual tourist track.

For a quieter, more immersive experience, spending a day on a local farm offers insight into Gozo's rural traditions. Many farms allow visitors to participate in activities such as olive picking, cheese-making, or harvesting seasonal fruits. These experiences provide a connection to the island's agricultural roots and the opportunity to taste truly fresh, organic produce straight from the source.

If you're looking for something even more offbeat, Gozo has a few hidden spots that offer stargazing experiences. With minimal light pollution, certain areas, especially near Ta' Cenc Cliffs, provide clear night skies that make for incredible stargazing opportunities. Some local guides even offer nighttime tours, where you can learn about constellations while soaking in the stillness of Gozo's countryside.

Quaint Villages and Walks

Gozo's charm lies in its slower pace of life, where tiny villages and scenic walks lead to stunning viewpoints, historic sites, and hidden gems far from the usual tourist crowds. Unlike the busier areas of Malta, Gozo's villages feel untouched, with their centuries-old stone buildings, quiet squares, and locals going about their day at a relaxed pace. Each village has its own personality, and walking through them offers a glimpse into the island's authentic side.

Għarb, one of the oldest villages on the island, is a perfect place to start. Its winding alleys and rustic limestone buildings transport you back in time. The village square is home to the Għarb Folklore Museum, which gives insight into Gozo's traditional way of life, from old farming tools to historic household objects. A walk through the village takes you past small chapels and family-run workshops where artisans craft pottery and lace, skills that have been passed down through generations. Just outside the village, the Ta' Pinu Basilica is an iconic pilgrimage site with stunning architecture and peaceful surroundings, making it an ideal place to pause and take in the quiet beauty of Gozo.

Xagħra, sitting on a hilltop, is another must-visit village. This spot is known for its prehistoric Ġgantija Temples, one of the oldest freestanding structures in the world, older than Stonehenge and the Pyramids of Egypt. A walk through Xagħra takes you past traditional townhouses with colorful wooden balconies, small bakeries selling fresh pastizzi, and the picturesque Xerri's Grotto, a lesser-known but stunning underground cave filled with stalactites and stalagmites. The village is also home to Ramla Bay, Gozo's most famous sandy beach, and if you take the scenic footpath leading down to the bay, you'll be rewarded with breathtaking coastal views.

Għasri is one of the quietest villages on the island, tucked away between the hills and fields of western Gozo. It's home to Wied il-Għasri, a narrow valley leading to a tiny pebbled cove, perfect for a refreshing swim after a walk through the countryside. The coastal trails from here lead toward Ta' Ġurdan Lighthouse, perched on a hill with some of the best panoramic views over the island and out to sea. The surrounding landscape is peaceful, with old farmhouses, dry stone walls, and a scattering of wildflowers in the cooler months.

Munxar and Sannat are two small villages that lead to some of Gozo's most dramatic landscapes. A walk from Sannat to Ta' Cenc Cliffs is a must for nature lovers, as the towering limestone cliffs drop dramatically into the sea below. The path winds past ancient cart ruts, wildflowers, and birdwatching spots, making it a perfect hike for those wanting to experience Gozo's wilder side. Munxar, just a short distance away, offers a quieter charm, with its sleepy streets and traditional stone houses.

Nadur, known for its citrus orchards and lively annual Carnival, is another great village to explore. It's also a gateway to some fantastic coastal walks, including paths leading down to San Blas Bay, a secluded beach with reddish-golden sand and crystal-clear waters. The walk is steep but rewarding, as the beach remains one of Gozo's most untouched spots. Another scenic route from Nadur takes you toward Dahlet Qorrot, a small fishing cove where you can see traditional boat sheds carved into the rock.

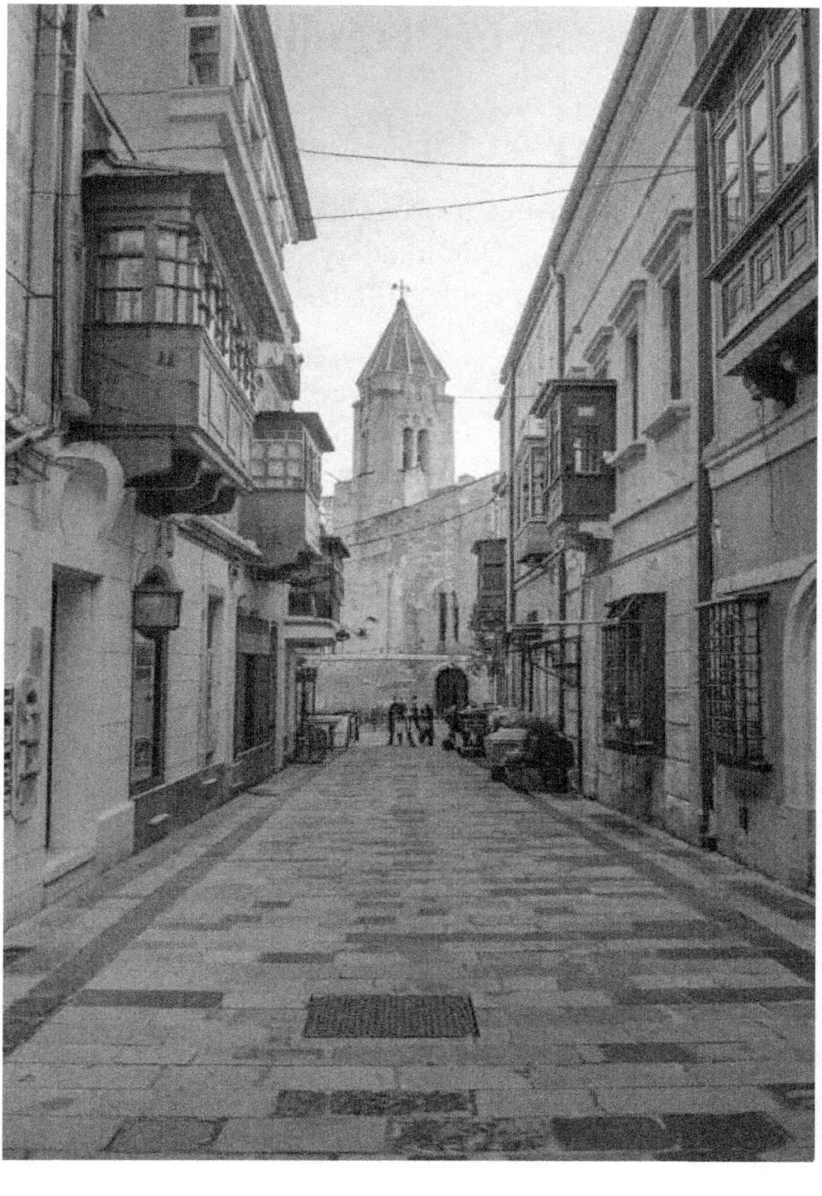

Trip Planning

7-Day Itinerary for First-Timers

Gozo may be small, but it offers the perfect mix of history, nature, and relaxation. This itinerary ensures you experience the island's highlights while still leaving time to enjoy its laid-back atmosphere.

Start your trip in Victoria, the heart of Gozo. Spend the morning exploring the Cittadella, the historic fortified city that offers panoramic views of the island. Walk through the Old Prison, Gozo Cathedral, and the Gozo Museum of Archaeology to get a sense of Gozo's past. After lunch at a café in Independence Square, visit the Ta' Pinu Basilica, a short drive away. This pilgrimage site is one of the most beautiful churches in the country and offers a peaceful atmosphere. In the evening, enjoy dinner at Il-Kartell in Marsalforn, known for its fresh seafood.

Head to Ġgantija, one of the world's oldest freestanding structures, predating the Pyramids of Egypt. After exploring the temples, take a short walk to the Ta' Kola Windmill, an 18th-century mill that provides insight into Gozo's rural life. Spend the afternoon wandering around Xagħra, stopping at Xerri's Grotto or Ninu's Cave to see underground rock formations. If you're in the mood for a beach break, Ramla Bay, with its distinctive red sand, is just a short drive away. Wrap up the day with dinner at Latini in Xagħra, a cozy spot serving local specialties.

Gozo's coastline is best explored on foot. Start your morning with a scenic hike along the Ta' Cenc Cliffs, where dramatic limestone formations drop into the sea. Follow the trails toward Sanap Cliffs, a quieter but equally stunning area. In the afternoon, head to San Blas Bay, a hidden gem with clear waters and golden-red sand. Getting there requires a short but steep walk, but the peaceful atmosphere makes it worth the effort. For an even more remote experience, visit Dahlet Qorrot, a tiny cove where fishermen still store their boats in caves carved into the rock. Have dinner at The View in Xlendi, which lives up to its name with stunning seaside views.

Dwejra Bay is home to some of Gozo's most famous landscapes. Start with the Inland Sea, a lagoon connected to the open Mediterranean by a natural rock tunnel. Take a short boat ride through the tunnel for breathtaking views of the rugged coastline. Nearby, the Blue Hole is one of Gozo's top diving sites, but even non-divers will appreciate the crystal-clear waters and dramatic rock formations. Walk along the coastline to visit Fungus Rock and the remains of the

Azure Window, where the collapsed structure still creates a striking scene. In the late afternoon, visit Wied il-Mielaħ, another natural rock arch that remains a quieter alternative to the more famous coastal landmarks. For dinner, head to Il-Kantra, a seaside restaurant tucked away in a peaceful cove near Mgarr ix-Xini.

Spend the next day discovering Gozo's rural charm. Drive to Għarb, one of the oldest villages on the island, and stroll through its quiet streets. Stop by the Għarb Folklore Museum to see artifacts from Gozo's past, then visit local workshops where artisans still produce pottery and lace by hand. From here, drive to Ta' Ġurdan Lighthouse for one of the best panoramic views of the island. After a light lunch in a traditional bakery, visit Wied il-Għasri, a narrow valley leading to a tiny pebbled cove, perfect for a peaceful swim. In the evening, enjoy a relaxed meal at Ta' Rikardu, a family-run restaurant inside the Cittadella, known for its Gozitan cheese and traditional dishes.

A day on the water offers a different perspective of the island. Take a boat trip around Comino, stopping at the famous Blue Lagoon. Though it's a popular spot, visiting early in the morning or later in the afternoon helps avoid the crowds. The lesser-known Crystal Lagoon is just as beautiful, with clearer waters and fewer people. After exploring the coastline, stop at

Santa Marija Bay, a quieter beach on Comino that offers a more relaxed atmosphere. Returning to Gozo in the afternoon, unwind with a sunset drink at Gleneagles Bar in Mgarr, where you can watch the boats come and go from the harbor.

On your final day, slow down and enjoy Gozo's laid-back atmosphere. Wander through Nadur, a village known for its citrus orchards and picturesque views, stopping at a local café for a leisurely breakfast. Take a short drive to Xlendi and walk along the scenic cliffs, or, if you're feeling adventurous, rent a kayak and explore the caves along the coastline. Spend the afternoon browsing for souvenirs in Victoria, picking up local delicacies like Gbejniet cheese, olive oil, and honey from the markets. End your trip with a relaxed meal at Tmun in Mgarr, where you can enjoy fresh seafood with a view of the harbor, reflecting on a week well spent exploring Gozo.

Family-Friendly Activities

Gozo and Malta offer a fantastic mix of family-friendly activities, from outdoor adventures to cultural experiences that cater to kids of all ages. Whether you're exploring historical sites, enjoying the beach, or discovering hands-on attractions, both islands provide plenty of opportunities for a fun and educational trip.

Start in Valletta, where history comes alive with interactive museums and impressive fortifications. The Malta Experience, an audio-visual show, gives a fascinating overview of Malta's past in a way that keeps kids engaged. Walk along the Upper Barrakka Gardens, where children can watch the daily cannon firing at the Saluting Battery while enjoying sweeping views of the Grand Harbour. Just outside the capital, Esplora Interactive Science Centre in Kalkara is one of the best attractions for families. It offers hands-on exhibits, a planetarium, and outdoor play areas, making science fun and accessible.

For a mix of history and adventure, Mdina, the Silent City, is a must-visit. Its narrow, winding streets feel like something out of a fairy tale, and kids will love exploring the old city walls. Nearby, the Mdina Dungeons offer a slightly spooky but fascinating look at Malta's medieval history. For animal lovers, The Mdina Glass Factory allows children to watch artisans at work, shaping colorful glass pieces that make for unique souvenirs.

A visit to Popeye Village in Anchor Bay is a highlight for young children. Originally built as the film set for the 1980 Popeye movie, it has since become a family-friendly attraction with activities, boat rides, and water trampolines. Not far from there, Golden Bay and Għajn Tuffieħa offer beautiful sandy beaches perfect for a relaxing day of swimming, sandcastle building, and exploring nearby cliffs.

In Gozo, the Cittadella in Victoria provides an exciting mix of history and exploration, with medieval walls to climb and small museums that introduce kids to Gozo's past. After exploring the fortress, a stop at Villa Rundle Gardens allows children to unwind in a shaded green space with playgrounds and fountains.

A beach day at Ramla Bay in Gozo is perfect for families, with its shallow waters and soft red sand. Older kids will enjoy the short hike up to Calypso's Cave, which offers fantastic views over the bay. If you prefer a more secluded setting, San Blas Bay provides a quieter alternative with crystal-clear waters.

For hands-on experiences, L-Arka Ta' Noe Animal Park in Xewkija lets kids interact with farm animals like rabbits, ponies, and goats. Another fantastic spot is Ta' Mena Estate, where families can learn about traditional Gozitan farming, taste fresh local produce, and even take part in activities like olive picking or cheese making.

Gozo's coastline offers plenty of adventure. The Dwejra Inland Sea is a fun spot for kids, where a short boat ride through a rock tunnel leads to a hidden cove with crystal-clear waters. Older children and teenagers can try snorkeling in the Blue Hole, one of the island's best diving sites.

For active families, Gozo's coastal trails are a great way to explore the island on foot. The walk from Xlendi to Kantra Bay is scenic but not too difficult for children. Another fun way to explore is by renting bikes and cycling through Gozo's quiet back roads, passing through charming villages and open countryside.
Evenings in Gozo and Malta can be just as enjoyable. In Marsalforn, kids can enjoy an ice cream while parents relax at a seaside café. The promenade is a great place for an evening stroll, with plenty of space for children to run around. In Malta, Sliema's waterfront promenade offers a similar experience, with parks, playgrounds, and views of Valletta across the harbor.

Conclusion

Malta and Gozo offer an experience that goes beyond sightseeing. These islands are a blend of ancient history, breathtaking landscapes, and vibrant local traditions, each leaving a lasting impression on those who visit. Whether you've wandered through the fortified streets of Valletta, explored the prehistoric temples of Ġgantija, swam in the crystal-clear waters of the Blue Lagoon, or simply enjoyed a quiet sunset over Ta' Cenc Cliffs, the essence of Malta and Gozo is found in the way they make you feel—welcomed, intrigued, and always wanting more.

The magic of these islands isn't just in their famous landmarks but in the small moments: the scent of fresh pastizzi from a village bakery, the sound of church bells echoing through a narrow alley, the warmth of a local sharing a story over a glass of Bajtra liqueur. Whether you've come for adventure, relaxation, or to uncover layers of history, Malta and Gozo reward you with experiences that stay with you long after you leave.

Traveling here is about more than ticking off a list of sights; it's about immersing yourself in the Mediterranean way of life—slow mornings by the sea, afternoons spent exploring limestone villages, and evenings filled with good food, good company, and the feeling of timelessness that these islands evoke. No matter how long you stay, Malta and Gozo have a way of making you feel at home while also leaving you with the urge to return.

Printed in Dunstable, United Kingdom